TEACH YOURSELF BOOKS

VISUALIZATION

Acknowledgement

I would like to thank my sister, Patricia Jackson, for compiling the index for this book.

VISUALIZATION

Pauline Wills

TEACH YOURSELF BOOKS

Long-renowned as the authoritative source for self-guided learning – with more than 30 million copies sold worldwide – the Teach Yourself series includes over 200 titles in the fields of languages, crafts, hobbies, sports, and other leisure activities.

Library of Congress Catalog Card Number: 96–68483

First published 1994 as *Visualisation: Headway Lifeguides*.
Re-published 1995 as *Visualisation for Beginners*.
Re-published in 1996 as *Teach Yourself Visualization*.

Catalogue entry for this title is available from the British Library.

First published in US 1996 by NTC Publishing Group, 4255 West Touhy Avenue, Lincolnwood (Chicago) Illinois 60646 – 1975 U. S. A.

The 'Teach Yourself' name and logo are registered trade marks of Hodder & Stoughton Ltd.

Typeset by Wearset, Boldon, Tyne and Wear.
Printed in Great Britain by Cox & Wyman, Reading, Berkshire.

Impression number	10	9	8	7	6	5	4	3	2	1
Year		2000	1999	1998	1997	1996				

CONTENTS

INTRODUCTION

As human beings, we are not just a physical body, but comprise body, mind and spirit. In order to be healthy and have optimum energy, these three aspects of our being have to work together, in harmony.

The human body is a very wonderful and self-healing instrument, given the right conditions. Unfortunately, many people have been conditioned into thinking that if they are unwell, they must visit their doctor for pills or medicine to eradicate the symptoms that have arisen. In doing this, the responsibility for one's own health is taken away. All that one has to do is to remember to take the prescribed medicine at set times during the day or night. How unlike our forefathers who learned to listen to their body and, if it became sick, rested and treated themselves through fasting and with herbs.

If our body becomes sick, it is usually because we are treating it in the wrong way. This could be through a poor diet, lack of exercise and a general lack of consideration. Whatever the cause, if this is not eradicated, the body will not return to optimum health.

What we often deny is the fact that the body, mind and spirit form a network of complex energies that are constantly interacting with each other. This means that we cannot separate these three parts of our being. The state of our mind affects our body, and the state of our body affects our mind. People who have been given placebos, believing that they are a new drug formulated to cure the disease that they have contracted, start to recover. As soon as they realise the truth, they go into relapse. The spirit is that divine part of us that has no beginning and no ending; that inner voice which, if we ask and listen to, will guide us on to our correct path in life and provide us, when the time is right, with the answers to our questions.

Visualization can play a very important role when working with the body and mind relationship. Frequently, visualization and imagination are likened to the same thing. This is not so. If one looks up the word visualization in a dictionary, the definition given is 'to call up a clear visual image'. The definition of imagination is: 'the faculty of forming images in the mind'. Though the difference is very slight, it is still quite distinct.

When first starting to work with visualization, it is normally the imagination that comes into play. Visualization usually takes time and practice to acquire. The exercises given in this book will use both visualization and imagination because both are equally important. If the mind can produce disease in the body, then the mind, through positive thinking and visualization, can eradicate it. I believe that disease is the body's way of telling us to stop and look at ourselves, and the path that we are treading. This normally indicates change, which may not be easy but is necessary for our own growth and understanding, and for the freedom of our spirit to find its source of origin.

1

WORKING WITH VISUALIZATION

When working with visualization, it is important that one practises regularly. Like any discipline, the more one works with it, the greater the results and benefits. In the beginning, it may seem very hard and the mind will create many reasons for not practising. This is where the first lesson is learnt, namely that we now have to be the master of our mind and emotions and not allow them to control us.

Try to practise at the same time each day. By doing this, it will become a habit, hopefully an enjoyable one. It is so easy to start the day with good intentions, promising oneself to work with the visualization techniques as soon as breakfast is over and everyone has left the house, for example. When the house is empty, one remembers that there is shopping to do but, after completing this chore, then time will be made. The shopping completed, someone calls or telephones, then something else happens and so the end of the day arrives and one is too tired to practise. Anyway, the end of the day is not an ideal time because of the temptation to fall asleep. The setting aside of a regular time each day, apart from establishing a discipline, creates a space, a space for oneself, which after a time becomes sacred.

In the world in which we live, with its noise, demands, stress and fast pace, we all need to find space for ourselves. Initially, this involves finding time each day to be alone, to do the things that we enjoy doing and not those which we are under obligation to do. It is a space where we can relax, reflect upon and work with ourselves. Initially, this space can be anywhere where we can be alone. It can be in the garden, the countryside, the park, where we live, or just sitting in the car. Eventually, what we are aiming for, and visualization works with this, is to find our own inner space – that quiet and peaceful inner state into which we can retreat in order to be unaffected by the noise and turmoil of daily living. In order to do this, we first have to learn the art of silence and peace.

When embarking upon this journey, it is important to be patient with yourself. Remember the familiar saying 'Rome was not built in a day': this equally applies to you. Be patient, and what you seek will be shown to you.

——— Simple starting techniques ———

When you have decided which part of the day you are going to reserve for yourself, find a place that is quiet and warm and where you will not be disturbed. Return to the same place each day. By doing this, good, positive vibrations will accumulate and saturate your chosen place. These vibrations will not only help you, but will also create an atmosphere of peace and tranquillity. You can place treasured objects around you, have comfortable cushions to lie on, or sit upon your favourite chair, if this is what you prefer. If you have a small portable tape recorder, have this to hand with some of your favourite relaxing music. You may like to burn incense or aromatherapy oils. Whatever creates an atmosphere of peace for you is beneficial to use.

If you smoke, it is advisable not to have a cigarette for at least two hours prior to your practice session. The reason for this is that it can interfere with some of the breathing techniques. Likewise, do not practise immediately after a main meal. The body is busy digesting food, which can make you sleepy.

Try to prevent any disturbance through noise. If you have a telephone, take the receiver off. If this is not possible, prepare yourself for the event of the doorbell or the telephone ringing so that you do not receive a shock. Wear clothes that are loose and comfortable to preclude restriction of the physical body and thereby restriction of the mind.

It is beneficial if you start your practice with relaxation because this relaxes the mind as well as the body and promotes easier concentration.

1   **Start your relaxation by lying down on the floor with a
    pillow beneath your head.** It is advisable to cover yourself
    with a blanket to keep warm, because when the body goes into
    a relaxed state, the metabolism slows down. Make sure that
    your body is straight, with your chin tucked in to prevent any
    strain on the back of your neck. Place your legs slightly apart,
    allowing your feet to fold outwards. Rest your arms on the floor
    approximately six inches away from your body, with the palms
    of your hands facing up towards the ceiling.

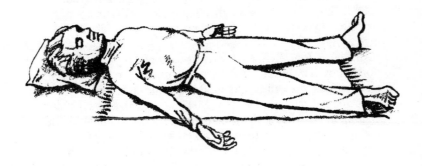

If you suffer with back problems, place your legs over a chair.
This prevents any strain in the lumbar spine.

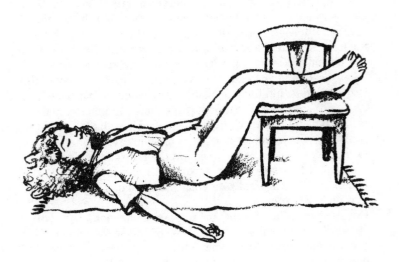

2 **When you are lying comfortably, start your relaxation by watching the thoughts that come into your mind.** Look at these thoughts and then, like beautiful bubbles, let go of them, allowing them to float into the atmosphere and gently disperse.

3 **As your mind starts to quiet and still, allow your concentration to be focused on your physical body.** Start with your feet; feel for any tension in your feet; try to release this tension in order that your feet can become relaxed and heavy.

4 **From your feet, move up both of your legs.** Feel your calves, shins, knees and thighs. Search for any tension in the muscles of your legs and then gently let go of it. Allow your legs to relax.

5 **From your legs bring your awareness into your abdomen.** Try to visualize the pelvic girdle, the lower spine and the muscles which surround this bone structure. If you are conscious of any tension, gently let go of it. Move inside your abdomen, visualizing the organs that are contained within the abdominal cavity. Try to locate any tension in this part of your body, gently releasing it in order that the whole of the abdomen may relax. When we are in a state of tension, it does not affect just the muscles, it affects every organ and all the systems within the physical body.

6 **From your abdomen, move up the body to your solar plexus.** Owing to the ganglia of nerve endings, it is the solar plexus which is affected when we experience fear, hence the saying 'butterflies in the stomach'. Also, the vagus nerve, one of the longest in the body, which starts in the medulla of the brain and terminates in the muscles of respiratory passageways, lungs, oesophagus, heart, stomach, small intestine, most of the large intestine and the gall-bladder can, when over-activated, cause difficulty with breathing, palpitations, and abdominal pains, to name but a few. How many of us have had to pay constant visits to the lavatory prior to an interview or an examination? When we become aware of the cause of a problem, it becomes easier to work with, and finally to eliminate. Mentally feel your solar plexus and, if there is any tension, try to release it.

7 **From your solar plexus, bring your awareness into your chest.** Try to visualize your sternum or breastbone; your ribcage and your thoracic spine. From your spine, feel the muscles that surround and support the skeletal bones of your

chest. Feel for any tension in these muscles, gently working with this tension in order to release it. Mentally, see inside your chest. Feel the gentle and rhythmic beat of your heart; remember that your heart is also a muscular organ and therefore prone to tension. Be conscious of the gentle inhalation and exhalation of your breath. Watch how your chest rises with each in breath and falls with each out breath. As you inhale concentrate on your diaphragm, the large muscle that divides your chest from your abdomen. Visualize this muscle stretching down into your abdomen as your lungs inflate and returning to its normal position with the deflation of the lungs during exhalation. Allow this movement to release the diaphragm from tension.

8 **From your chest let your concentration travel across your shoulders and down both of your arms into your hands and fingers.** If there is tension in this part of your body, try to relax it.

9 **From your hands come back to your neck.** Relax your throat and all the muscles around your neck. A cause of headaches can be the accumulation of tension around the shoulders and the neck. Relax this part of your body and allow it to become heavy and at rest.

10 **From your neck, move into your head.** Relax your tongue, jaw, cheeks, eyes, forehead and the back of your head. Feel as though your head is sinking into the ground.

11 **Lastly, bring your concentration into the whole of your body.** If you still feel that there is tension, gently try to release it. For most people, tension is the norm. Therefore, to replace this with relaxation takes time and practice. Do not be disheartened if you do not succeed immediately. Practice and patience will render positive results. Each time you practise this or any of the other techniques given further on in the book, you should be able to achieve a deeper and longer-lasting state of relaxation.

12 **When coming out of relaxation, gently start to move your feet; then flex the muscles in your legs; gently move your fingers; breathing in, raise your arms up over your head, stretching the whole of your body.** Breathing out, bring your arms back down to your sides. Repeat this twice more, then open your eyes and slowly roll over on to your left side and sit up.

Each time you put yourself into relaxation, or practise any of the visualization techniques given in this book, try to be aware of how they affect you mentally, emotionally and physically. You can either do this from memory or keep a notebook nearby in order to write down your experiences. It can be very encouraging to look back over the notes you have made in order to discover how far you have progressed.

When working with visualization techniques it is important to have a positive attitude towards them. If you are working with a stress problem or with some form of disease and you doubt the efficacy of the technique that you are using, then it most probably will not work for you. Remember that the mind affects the body. We all have times of doubt and find ourselves thinking negatively. When this happens, we have to try to reverse the situation by turning the doubt into trust and negative attitudes into positive ones.

In the beginning this can be quite difficult because we have to become aware of our thought patterns. To do this can be quite revealing. During the course of a day try to be consciously aware of what you are thinking. Make an effort to stop and review what has been passing through your mind. If you find that there is any negativity, change it into the positive. If you find yourself thinking that you will not recover from a particular disease or not be able to solve the problem that confronts you, tell yourself that you will return to optimum health and that the problem will solve itself in such a way that everything works for the best.

All thoughts create forms or shapes that not only surround us but are also projected out into the atmosphere. Like attracts like, therefore negative or positive thoughts will attract others of a like nature. Learning to look at negativity and reversing it to the positive is one of the first steps in visualization.

One of the first questions that I always put to my students is how much are they able to love themselves. This is usually followed by laughter and the answer: 'we don't'. I have had students tell me that to love oneself is very selfish and wrong. My reply is; if we are unable to love ourselves, are we truly able to love others?

When we truly love ourselves, we become love, which radiates out from our whole being. We then no longer have to think about loving others, we do it automatically. Truly loving ourselves incorporates every part of us, not just our physical body. It involves loving our feelings, our thoughts and that divine part of us that has no beginning and no ending. Loving ourselves enables us to laugh at our mistakes and idiosyncracies, and thereby teaches us to learn by them. It also teaches us humility.

An exercise that I ask my students to do in order to help them to start loving themselves is to look at their reflection in a mirror first thing in the morning and last thing at night and to say out loud to that reflection; I love you, I love you, I love you. Again, this is usually followed by laughter, but those students who faithfully carry out this simple procedure often say that wonderful things start to happen to them. May I suggest that you, the reader, try this for yourself in order to discover what changes it renders in you.

Tratakam

One of the easiest ways of experiencing visualization is through the practice of **tratakam**, which translated means 'clearing the vision'. Tratakam is one of the **kriyas** or cleansing techniques used in yoga. The *Hatha Yoga Pradipika*, an acknowledged text on yoga, claims that tratakam can cure all diseases of the eyes. Prior to the practice of tratakam, it is recommended that certain eye exercises are practised. Not only will these strengthen the eyes, but will also enable a steady, unwavering vision to be achieved. This is an important aid to visualization because a focused vision brings about a focused mind. It is only when the mind is focused that we are able to transcend it to reach into the higher levels of consciousness. For anyone who has weak eyes, the two following exercises should be practised daily.

Eye Exercise 1

1 Sit comfortably at the end of a well-lit room and look at the far wall. Keeping your head perfectly still, allow your eyes to travel along the horizontal lines where the floor and ceiling meet. Now, move your eyes diagonally from corner to corner, then lastly around the outline of the wall, first clockwise and then anticlockwise.

2 Keeping your gaze fixed on a chosen point, move your head firstly from side to side, then up and down, and lastly round in circles.

3 Hold the tips of the index fingers of both hands together at eye level and at reading distance from them. Look at the point where the fingers meet and then look through this point into the distance. You should notice the appearance of a third finger as your vision extends, which disappears as you bring your vision back to the junction of the two fingers.

Eye Exercise 2

Keeping your head perfectly still, perform each of the following movements ten times, firstly in a clockwise direction and then in an anticlockwise direction.

1 Roll your eyes to the extreme top of the socket. Hold for one second.

2 Roll your eyes to the extreme right of the socket and hold for one second.

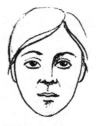

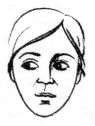

3 Roll your eyes to the extreme bottom of the socket and hold for one second.

4 Roll your eyes to the extreme left of the socket and hold for one second.

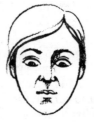

Tratakam visualization 1

To practise tratakam you will need a candle and a box of matches. Initially it is advantageous to practise this technique either in a darkened room or after sunset.

Sit in a dark place that is quiet and warm, where you will not be disturbed. Place the lighted candle about three feet in front of you. Concentrate your gaze upon the flame without blinking. When your eyes start to water or get tired, close them. What is important is that you do not induce eye strain. In front of your closed eyes should appear the flame of the candle. It will most probably move around before finally disappearing. When it disappears, try to bring the flame back into focus. If nothing happens, repeat the exercise by opening your eyes and gazing once more at the flame. The aim of the exercise is to hold the image of the flame before your closed eyes, keeping it perfectly still for as long as possible.

Tratakam visualization 2

A second visualization exercise using the flame of a candle works towards finding your own inner centre of peace and tranquillity. Start this exercise in the same way as visualization 1. When you close your eyes and the image of the flame appears, try to hold it still. After a few moments, visually take the flame from in front of your closed eyes to the middle of your chest. It is here that your heart centre is located. Now visualize the flame becoming larger until it fills the whole of your chest cavity with a pale magenta light, the colour of spiritual love. Allow the magenta light to radiate out from your chest until it forms an orb of light around you. Let the love which permeates this colour suffuse the whole of your being, filling you with peace and tranquillity.

When you are ready, visualize the flame returning to its normal size and then take its image back to your closed eyes. Gently open your eyes, still retaining that inner peace and love.

What you have experienced with the candle flame, you are working towards experiencing with all objects used in visualization. With regular practice, the peace and tranquillity that you experience will intensify, and the length of time that you are able to maintain it will grow.

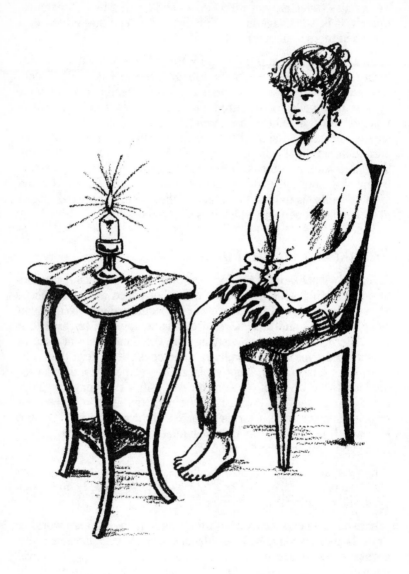

2

THE BREATH

'Life is in the breath; therefore he who only half breathes, half lives'. This yogic proverb attempts to impress upon us that the way in which we breathe directly affects our physical and mental well-being and determines to a great extent the length and quality of our lives.

It is a medical fact that we can live without food for many weeks, and without water and sleep for several days, but we are only able to live without air for a few minutes. Air is a simple gaseous mixture of approximately 20 per cent oxygen, 78 per cent nitrogen and 1 per cent argon, with other rarer gases. It also contains a substance called **prana**, or universal energy.

Prana

Pranayama is the yogic science of the control of prana in the human body. Pranayama is derived from the words **prana** and **ayama**. The translation of ayama is length, expansion, retention and control. On a bright sunny day, prana can be seen as minute specks of brilliant light. It is in great abundance in the atmosphere when the sun is shining, it decreases on dull, cloudy days and it is greatly reduced after dark.

Pranayama is the most vital of sciences because all energies which manifest in the form of life are pranic. If we are able to intensify and consciously control pranic metabolism, it will result in multiplying our physical and mental energies. By doing this, we experience a greater sense of well-being and improved health. We exist by constantly drawing prana from the cosmos. This extraction takes place through the skin, the tongue and the air cells in our lungs.

Our skin is one of the largest and most important organs of the body. Without it, we cannot survive. This has been proven through severe burn cases. As well as being a waterproof envelope of protection, toxins, which would otherwise accumulate in the body, are eliminated through the pores of the skin. In order for the skin to absorb pranic energy, it should be in contact with the air. This is not always possible in winter. If we are able to expose the skin for a short duration to sunlight, then a large quantity of prana or life-force is absorbed. Having said this, I am aware of the dangers of long exposure to the sun and am not recommending this. All things should be practised in moderation. Have you noticed how energised you feel when you are able to be out in the open and the sunshine? The ideal clothing to wear is that which is made from natural fibres such as cotton, silk or pure wool. Man-made fibres prevent the body from breathing and prevent absorption of prana.

Visualization for a sunny day

On a warm sunny day, sit in the sun either in a park or in the peace of the countryside. Whichever place you choose, make sure that it is quiet and free from the noise and pollution of traffic.

If possible, sit on the grass, making sure that your spine is straight and your body relaxed. If your prefer you can lie down. Start your visualization by relaxing your mind. Watch all the thoughts that are constantly bombarding it and, visualizing them as beautiful bubbles, allow them to be released into the atmosphere where they gently disperse. When you have stilled your mind, bring your concentration into your physical body and feel the warmth of the sun's rays upon it. Try to visualize the space that surrounds you filled with tiny brilliant white specks of dancing, vibrating, prana. As you inhale, visualize these tiny specks passing through the thousands of pores in your skin and entering your body. As well as being able to breathe through the nose and mouth, you are able to breathe through any part of your body. See your body becoming filled with pulsating energy, which revitalises every cell and atom. If you are experiencing pain in a particular area of your body, consciously direct this pranic energy to it. Feel any pain being released and any disharmony being reharmonised.

When you are ready, breathe in, bringing your arms up over your head in order to stretch the whole of your body. As you breathe out, bring your arms back down to your sides. Repeat this twice more before opening your eyes. If you are lying on the grass, roll over onto your right side and sit up.

Visualization on eating

A considerable part of the body's energy is extracted from food. How many times have you heard the saying 'You are what you eat'? If we view vegetables and fruits as concentrated solar energy, then eating the right food in the right way will supply us with abounding vigour and vitality. Prana from food is absorbed not so much by the stomach and intestines as by the tongue. Therefore, the longer we are able to chew our food before swallowing it, the greater will be the absorption of prana. Yogis advocate that food should be chewed until none of its natural taste remains because they believe that this occurrence is a sign that all of the prana has been absorbed and what is left, namely food bulk, is used as building material by the body.

For this exercise, you will require an apple.

Sit down in the place that you have chosen for your practice. Take the apple into both of your hands and observe it. Look at its overall colour and shape. Take note of any variations in these. Perhaps parts of the apple are more green or more red than other parts. Look at the stem that joined the apple to the tree. Closing your eyes try to visualize the apple, firstly as you saw it in your hands and then filled with glowing pranic energy. This should turn your apple into a ball of white light.

When you have achieved this, open your eyes and take a bite out of the apple. As you chew, close your eyes, becoming aware of the process of mastication. Take note of the apple's flavour. Start to visualize the apple in your mouth reverting back to pranic energy. See each tiny piece as a particle of white light which is absorbed into your body through your tongue. Allow this energy to revitalise and reharmonise your body, mind and spirit. When all the flavour from the apple has gone, swallow what remains in order that it may be used to repair and rebuild your body.

Each time that you practise this exercise, try using a different fruit or vegetable. At first, you may find that your jaw aches through prolonged chewing, but after a while, the muscles of the jaw will become stronger, eliminating the ache.

The respiratory system

The respiratory system, through which we take in air and prana, is a wonderful and precise system. It is divided into the upper respiratory tract consisting of the nose, mouth, sinus cavities, throat and larynx, and the lower respiratory tract consisting of the trachea, the bronchi and the lungs. The lungs, which are the principal organs of the respiratory system, are situated in the upper part of the thoracic cage and comprise the bronchial tubes, bronchioles and alveoli or air sacs.

When we inhale, we take in air through our nose. The nose conditions the air that we breathe by freeing it from dust, warming it and

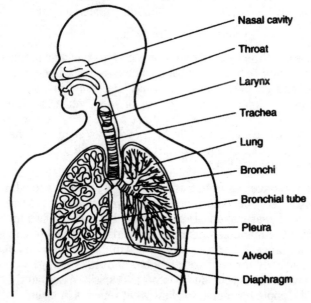

Nasal cavity

Throat

Larynx

Trachea

Lung

Bronchi

Bronchial tube

Pleura

Alveoli

Diaphragm

The respiratory system

moistening it. If you run down the road on a cold winter day, breathing through your mouth, it can be quite painful as the cold air enters the lungs. It has also been shown through surgery that people who smoke cigarettes and inhale the smoke through their mouth, have dark brown lungs instead of the normal pink colour.

The nasal cavities are filled with an infinite number of ultra sensitive nervous receptors that give us our sense of smell. Compared with animals, this sense is atrophied. From the air, animals can pick up the scent of danger, the location of food and water and the scent of females, often many miles away. Tribes, who live close to nature, still have the acute sense of smell that is present in the animal kingdom.

From the nose, the warmed, clean and moistened air passes down the larynx, into the trachea, which then divides into two main bronchi, one for each lung. Within the lung, each bronchus then divides into increasingly smaller bronchioles. At the tip of all bronchioles are balloon-like cavities called alveoli. The vital exchange of oxygen for carbon dioxide occurs through minute blood vessels in the thin alveoli walls.

NOTE

Certain breathing techniques can be dangerous unless carried out under supervision, therefore they should not be experimented with. The breathing visualizations given in this chapter are perfectly safe if the given instructions are adhered to.

When practising breathing techniques, if at any time you become breathless, immediately return to normal breathing. Breathlessness is a sign that there is a build-up of carbon dioxide which your body is trying to get rid of by making you breathe more quickly. Likewise, if you start to feel dizzy, again revert to normal breathing. Dizziness is a sign that you are hypoventilating. With practice, you will become accustomed to taking in greater volumes of oxygen at a slower rate thus eliminating any feeling of dizziness.

The principal muscle concerned with respiration is the diaphragm. This large dome-shaped muscle divides the chest cavity from the abdomen. When air is sucked in, the diaphragm contracts, along with other muscles between the ribs; when the muscles relax, air is forced up the respiratory tract and out of the body by the elastic recoil of the lungs.

Most of us only use about one-third of our lung capacity. If we are able to utilise them fully we are able to energise the body more efficiently.

Visualization on the breath

Sit down either on the floor or on a chair in your chosen practice space. Make sure that your spine is straight and your shoulders are down and slightly back. This ensures that your chest is expanded and open, allowing room for the inflated lungs.

When your body is relaxed and comfortable, bring your concentration to the tip of your nose. Feel the cool air entering your nostrils as you inhale and the warm air as you exhale. After three to four minutes of practising this, move to the next stage.

Using your imagination, follow the air's route from your nose into your trachea; from your trachea into the two bronchi that lead into

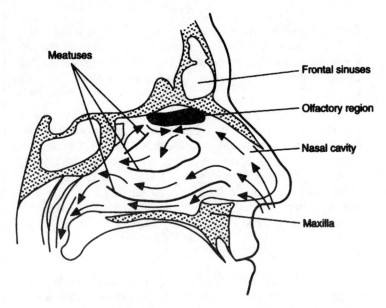

The passageways of the meatuses

the bronchioles, and finally into the alveoli which make up the lungs. Try to visualize the exchange of oxygen for carbon dioxide and other waste gases through the capillaries in the alveoli walls. Now take these waste gases back along the same route to your nose in order to exhale them.

By practising this exercise you will familiarise yourself with the functioning of the respiratory system. This will greatly help when working with visualization techniques for lung disorders.

In order to breathe correctly during visualization exercises on the breath, it is important to know the structure of the nose. The air current that enters the nose is divided into three streams in each nostril by the groove-like passageways of the meatuses. In the olfactory region at the top of the nasal cavity, the direction of the air flow is reversed, bringing the air into contact with zones able to distinguish smells. In normal breathing, only a small percentage of the air comes into contact with the olfactory zone but it is possible, with practice, to direct a greater flow of air towards it. If we wish to absorb the maximum amount of prana from the intake of air, it is important to do this.

When watching animals trying to detect a particular smell, one notices that in the process of sniffing the nostrils, with the aid of the muscles on either side of the nose, are dilated. This modifies the shape of the funnel formed by the lower part of the nose, enabling the air to be directed to the area with the most sensitive nerve endings, namely the olfactory region. Because the olfactory region is also the region where prana is absorbed, a greater amount of this is taken into the body at the same time. Try practising this form of breathing with the next exercise.

Exercise on dilating the nostrils

1 Sitting comfortably with your spine straight, shoulders down and back, and your chest opened, firstly try contracting the small muscles on either side of your nose. Feel your nose dilating.
2 After performing this four or five times, dilate your nose and take in a deep breath. Release as you exhale. Now take in a deep breath without contracting your nose muscles. Try to feel the subtle differences. At first you may not notice anything, but with practice, your sense of smell should become more acute and, through the greater absorption of prana, your energy levels should increase.

3 If we wish to use the full capacity of our lungs, we have to learn how to take a complete breath, which is not the same as a deep breath. A complete breath involves all of the stale air being forced out of the lungs before the fresh air is drawn in.

Exercise 1 Deep inhalation, normal exhalation

1 Start the following three exercises by lying on the floor with one or two blankets folded lengthwise under the lumbar spine, chest and head. Place a third folded blanket under your head. This helps to open out the chest.

2 Firstly, relax for three to four minutes. Breathe out deeply in order to rid the lungs of stale air.
3 In a relaxed manner, inhale slowly, softly and deeply through both nostrils, aiming to lengthen the breath without strain. While inhaling, be conscious of the lungs and the front ribs expanding. When you feel that your lungs are full, breathe out normally without collapsing the ribcage.
4 Repeat six more times.

This breathing technique is beneficial for those suffering from lack of energy and low blood pressure.

Exercise 2 Normal inhalation, deep exhalation

1 Consciously relax the body for three to four minutes.
2 Breathe out deeply in order to rid the lungs of stale air.
3 Breathe in normally, then, without strain, slowly exhale. Control the outflow of breath, keeping it soft and smooth with no jerks. Let your awareness be on the breath throughout these exercises.

4 Repeat a further six times.

The practice of this breathing technique benefits high blood pressure and helps to bring a sense of peace and calm to the whole body.

Exercise 3   Deep inhalation and deep exhalation

1 Consciously relax the body for three to four minutes before breathing out deeply.
2 Take a long, slow and deep inhalation until you feel that the breath has reached your collarbones.
3 Keeping the chest lifted and open, exhale slowly and deeply, controlling the breath so that it is not jerky and guarding against putting strain on the throat.
4 Repeat six times.

The number of times these exercises are repeated can be increased over a period of weeks. What is important is that you do not at any time put strain upon your body. When you first begin to practise, if you find that you start to get out of breath before completing six rounds, then reduce it to four, or even three.

When you have mastered these techniques lying down, then you may practise them in a sitting posture. Whether you choose to sit on the floor or on a chair, it is important that your spine is straight and your chest open. Before starting, close your eyes and lower your head so that your chin moves down towards your chest. If you are sitting on a chair, a straight-backed one is preferable.

The major centre for the storage of life-force or prana is the solar plexus. This is located at the top of the abdomen, beneath the ribs. During respiration, prana collects in this area.

Visualization of Prana

1 Sitting either on a straight-backed chair or on the floor, relax your body, making sure that your spine is straight and your chest open. If you have chosen to sit on a chair, place the soles of both your feet on the floor and your hands on your knees.

2 Start this exercise by taking a few normal breaths, allowing your concentration to be centred in the breath. Then place all ten fingers lightly on your solar plexus. Exhale deeply to rid the lungs of stale air.

3 In a relaxed manner, inhale slowly, deeply and softly. During this inhalation, visualize the pranic energy as an intense white light. Visualize it entering your nostrils, moving downward into your solar plexus and passing into your fingertips. Slowly, and without strain, exhale. Repeat six to eight times.

4 If you are suffering from any disharmony in your physical body, the white pranic light can be transferred from your fingertips to the part of your body where it is needed.

Transferring pranic energy

1 Start this exercise as you did
   the previous one.
2 When you have completed
   the inhalation and visualized
   your fingers filled with white
   light, retain the breath while
   moving your fingers to the
   place where there is pain or
   discomfort.
3 Exhale very slowly,
   visualizing the white pranic
   light flowing from your
   fingertips into the chosen
   part of your body.
4 When the exhalation is
   complete, suspend the
   breath while you return your
   fingertips to your solar
   plexus.
5 Repeat from the inhalation,
   until the pain or discomfort
   has subsided. If you become
   breathless before this, then
   stop immediately, resuming
   normal breathing.

Pranic visualization standing

1 Come into a standing position with your feet slightly apart and
   your hands by your sides. (Figure 1, page 22)
2 Exhale deeply, allowing your chin to sink onto your chest as you
   do so.
3 As you take a deep and slow inhalation, start to raise your arms
   slowly, visualizing the white ball of pranic energy in the solar
   plexus becoming larger.
4 Continue the deep, slow inhalation and the slow raising of your
   arms, keeping your elbows straight. As your chest expands and
   as more air enters your lungs and more life-force fills your body,
   you become increasingly alive.

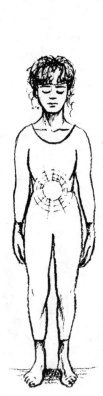

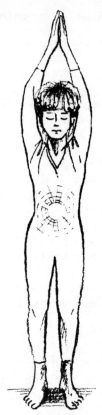

Figure 1 **Figure 2**

5 The inhalation becomes complete as the palms of your hands
   meet overhead. Retain the breath for a count of five while
   visualizing your body permeated with prana, and totally vitalised.
   (Figure 2)
6 Now begin a very slow exhalation, reversing the movements. As
   your arms are slowly lowered, the life-force gradually becomes
   depleted, leaving your body limp and relaxed. Try to feel and
   visualize this progressive depletion.
7 When the exhalation is complete and your hands are back by
   your sides, hold the breath out for a count of five before
   repeating.
8 This visualization technique can be performed up to eight times.
   Remember that the inhalation and exhalation must be slow and

controlled, otherwise it will not give you adequate time for visualization. Again, should you become out of breath, stop and resume normal breathing.

The nadis

Our physical body is surrounded by an electromagnetic field or aura. This will be explained more fully in a later chapter. One of the layers or sheaths which constitute the aura is known as the etheric double. This interpenetrates with, and is the blueprint for, the physical body. Situated in this sheath are the main energy centres or chakras and also the very fine energy channels or **nadis** through which pranic energy flows. This network of infinitely intricate nadis constitutes the counterpart of the entire nervous system which forms an important part of the human mechanism. The number of nadis are numerous. Some ancient documents purport there to be 72,000, others as many as 350,000.

In the text *Gorakshasataka of the Nath sect* the guru Goraknath states that among the thousands of nadis that serve as carriers of prana, seventy-two are said to be important. Of these, ten are particularly noteworthy. For the purpose of the following visualization techniques, only three of these need to be mentioned. These are Ida, Pingala and Sushumna.

In any electrical circuit, three specific wires are required for conduction: one positive, one negative and a third which is neutral. Likewise, within the body these three specific nadis are connected with conducting energy. **Pingala** is the positive line, which channels the dynamic energy of prana. It is associated with the sympathetic nervous system which releases adrenalin to stimulate the superficial muscles. The sympathetic nervous system prepares the body to cope with stress and external activity.

Ida is the negative line, the channel of mental force. It is connected with the parasympathetic nervous system which sends impulses to the visceral organs to stimulate the internal processes.

In order to avoid short-circuiting of these lines, there is a third channel that can function as an earth wire. This is the **sushumna**. But the real purpose of sushumna is to provide a channel for the

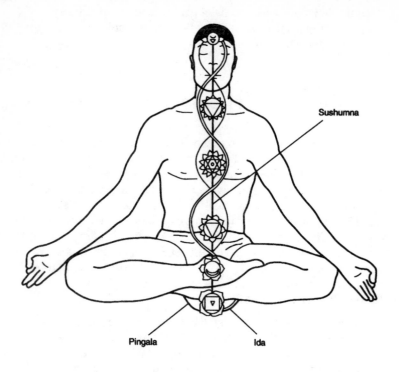

great spiritual energy force in man. When man is ready mentally, physically and spiritually, this force rises to bring about enlightenment or God consciousness.

Everywhere in the external world we encounter manifestations of the positive–negative principle. We find it in the composition of the atom, in the cell, in the polarity of the earth, in the sun and moon, and in the man and woman relationship. In those dimensions of existence which we gradually come to perceive through our inner vision, the same positive–negative relationship occurs. Just as we know that a certain balance must be maintained between the positive and negative ratio in the external world, likewise a constant balance must be maintained in the constant interplay of positive–negative pranic current. The breathing visualization technique that aids this is alternate nostril breathing or **sukh purvak**.

Alternate nostril breathing

1 Sit either on a chair or on the floor in your chosen place. Make sure that your spine is straight and your body relaxed.
2 Place your right thumb lightly against your **right** nostril; your index and middle finger together on your forehead, between and just above your eyebrows and your ring and little finger lightly against your **left** nostril.
3 Exhale deeply through both nostrils.
4 Press the **right** nostril closed with the thumb and quietly inhale deeply through the **left** nostril to a count of eight.
5 Keeping the **right** nostril closed, press the **left** nostril closed with your ring and little finger and retain the breath for a count of four.
6 Open the **right** nostril and exhale deeply through it to a count of eight.

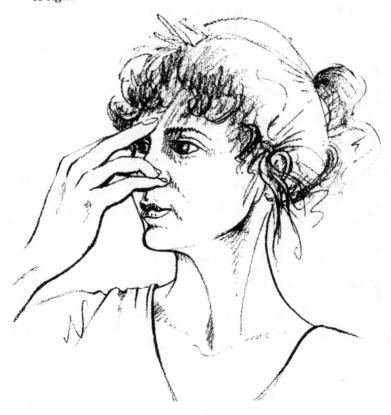

7 Without pausing, inhale through the **right** nostril to a rhythmic count of eight.

8 Press the **right** nostril closed with your thumb and retain the air for a count of four.

9 Open the **left** nostril and exhale deeply through it.

10 Without pausing, inhale through your **left** nostril to a count of eight.

SUMMARY

Inhale through left nostril for a count of eight.
Retain with both nostrils closed for a count of four.
Exhale through right nostril for a count of eight.

Without pause:

Inhale through right nostril for a count of eight.
Retain with both nostrils closed for a count of four.
Exhale through left nostril for a count of eight.

This completes one round. Without pausing, perform ten more rounds. When you have completed these, place your hands on your knees and breathe normally. Reflect on any changes which may have taken place mentally, physically or emotionally during this exercise.

Because the network of nadis constitutes the entire nervous system, alternate nostril breathing not only brings into balance the positive and negative flow of prana but it also relieves nervous tension and stress, bringing a sense of peace and quietness to the body, mind and emotions.

Visualizing white pranic light

When you have become familiar with the alternate nostril breath, bring into it visualization of white pranic energy. During each inhalation, visualize breathing in an intense white light. Allow this to circulate throughout all the nadis in order to cleanse and vitalise. When you exhale, visualize breathing out all disharmony and pain in the form of a grey mist.

Using the breathing exercises and visualizations in this chapter regularly should improve the health and vitality of your physical body.

Visualizations on the breath can be dynamic; they can be passive. They can restore energy and vitality to every atom and cell; they can bring relaxation, healing and peace; that perfect peace which passes all man's understanding.

3

STRESS

Stress is a mental and physical reaction to an outward situation, be this in the present, past or future. Owing to the chemical reactions that it produces in the physical body, if stress is prolonged or produced by more than one factor, it can lead to a physical and/or mental breakdown.

Our physical body is a wonderful instrument which, through the never ending environmental changes, constantly strives to bring about a state of equilibrium through homeostasis. Homeostasis is a condition in which the body's internal environment remains within certain physiological limits (homeo = same; stasis = standing still). An organism is said to be in homeostasis when its internal environment contains the optimum concentration of gases, nutrients, ions and water, has an optimal temperature and an optimal pressure for the health of the cells. The homeostatic responses of the body are subject to control by the nervous and endocrine systems. When homeostasis is disturbed, ill health may result.

Homeostasis in all organisms is continually disturbed by stress. Fortunately the body has many regulating devices that oppose the forces of stress and bring the body back into balance. But, if the body is weak because of poor diet, lack of sleep or exercise, or if the stress factor is prolonged and with more than one cause, the body may be unable to restore its equilibrium, resulting in a breakdown.

When we are faced with a stressful situation, the body is roused into action. Impulses are sent to the brain via the nervous system, which activates the pituitary gland to secrete hormones into the bloodstream. These hormones then activate the adrenal glands (our flight or fight glands) to secrete adrenaline and noradrenaline into the bloodstream. The effect of this is to increase the heart and respiratory rate, raise the blood pressure, make the stomach queasy and encourage the liver to secrete more glucose in order to promote energy to enable us to extricate ourselves from the impending danger. Our muscles tense, ready for action, and our immune system becomes less active, thereby subjecting us to a greater risk from infection. In a situation where, for example, we find ourselves in a field with a bull and have to move pretty rapidly in order to save ourselves from danger, the extra adrenaline, noradrenaline and glucose that has been produced, is utilised by the body through the act of running to escape danger. When under stress, these excess amounts of hormones that are released are not used and can, if these bodily reactions are continually repeated, become increasingly harmful, especially to people with heart disease.

Causes of stress

Stress can be induced by one or more factors. These include the death of a friend or loved one, divorce, illness, loss or change of job, retirement, change of home, tending an aged parent, pregnancy, burglary and financial problems. It can be due to external factors such as excessive noise, driving to and from work in heavy traffic each day, a boring or repetitive job, the boredom experienced by a woman who relinquishes an interesting and challenging occupation in order to tend the home and rear a family. Stress can equally be brought out by an inability to resolve past events, resulting in feelings of guilt and self-pity, or in the anticipation of future events such as the fear of sitting an exam, taking a driving test, or purely from fear of what the future holds for each one of us individually.

How we cope with stress differs with each person. Some people manage to be easygoing and relaxed, no matter what the stresses and pressures on them. For others, even a small problem becomes a major disaster, a source of constant worry or anger. If you are in the latter group, try to remember how strong emotions affect your body.

Your mental health

Realising the wear and tear that stress has on us physically, mentally and emotionally, it is important to have not just a healthy body but also a healthy mind. If you ask yourself if you are fit enough to avoid breaking down under emotional stress or strain, what would your answer be? To help you to evaluate your mental health, below are 16 questions. If you answer 'yes' to three or more questions, then it would be advisable to start looking at yourself and your lifestyle, trying to find ways to eliminate the stress that you are undergoing. Also try working with the visualizations given at the end of the questionnaire for some of the problems mentioned.

When working with a questionnaire, it is important to answer it truthfully and not from the vision of how you would like it to be – this causes an illusion which is self-deceptive and provides no help. It is only by being honest with ourselves that change can take place; change which initially aids our mental and emotional growth, and ultimately our growth as a complete human being.

QUESTIONNAIRE

Answer YES or NO to the following questions

1	Do you feel generally tired and lacking in energy?	YES/NO
2	Are you sleeping badly?	YES/NO
3	Do you find it difficult to mix with people?	YES/NO
4	Do you lack friends and close family ties?	YES/NO
5	Do you find it hard to concentrate on something even when you want to do so?	YES/NO
6	Are you bored with your job and not doing it to the best of your ability?	YES/NO
7	Do you lack other interests and activities outside of your work?	YES/NO
8	Do you find communicating with other people difficult?	YES/NO
9	Do trivial setbacks and inconveniences make you irritable?	YES/NO

10	Do you tend to neglect your personal appearance?	YES/NO
11	Do you view life as a continual uphill struggle?	YES/NO
12	Do you suffer frequent headaches?	YES/NO
13	When you think about the future, do you become depressed?	YES/NO
14	Do you find meals dull and boring?	YES/NO
15	Are you unhappy sexually?	YES/NO
16	Does the future look black?	YES/NO

- Visualizations for coping with stress -

Lack of energy

Go to the space that you have set aside for yourself and lie down in the relaxation posture described in chapter 1.

Try to relax your mind by looking at the constant stream of thoughts passing through it and gently letting go of them. When your mind has become quiet, bring your awareness into your physical body and try to assess the amount of tension that you are holding on to. Starting at your feet and working up to your head, try to relax your body by releasing this tension.

Now, bring your concentration into your breath. As you breathe in, visualize a shaft of magenta light entering through the top of your head, travelling down your spine and legs and passing out through your feet. Exhale. On the next inhalation, breathe in a shaft of green light through your feet, up through your spine and out through the top of your head. Exhale.

Continue to inhale the magenta and green lights alternatively for five to ten minutes. This will work on polarising your body.

When you have completed this, breathe in a shaft of golden light through your head and visualize it entering and revitalising every muscle, organ and cell of your body. When your body is full of golden light, allow this colour to extend beyond your physical body, forming a golden orb of protection around you. Relax in this orb of light for a further ten to fifteen minutes before bringing your body back to normal activity, as described in chapter 1.

Insomnia

If you are suffering from insomnia, try not to eat a heavy meal late at night; do not drink coffee or tea after 4 pm. These drinks are a stimulant and will help to keep you awake. Try to relax by working in the evening with your own creativity; through knitting, embroidery, painting or listening to music. If you enjoy reading, take a good book to bed with you and read until you start to feel drowsy.

After putting out the light, make sure that your body is comfortable and warm. Bless the day that has just passed and allow it to fade from your mind. This night you are turning over to a new page in your book of life, enabling you to start tomorrow afresh.

Be aware of the silence that night brings. Inhale this stillness and silence into your body. In so doing, your body begins to feel light and warm. Visualize your bed turning into a fluffy white cloud that gently lifts and floats you out into the clear night air. The night owl and other nocturnal creatures are the only souls about, on the prowl for food and sport. Snug and warm on your fluffy white cloud, you are able to see the myriad stars stretching far out into the universe. In the silence you perceive the sound that each star and planet makes, culminating into wondrous undulating harmonies. Becoming immersed into this glorious symphony, the mantle of sleep gently wraps herself around you allowing your physical body to become repaired and re-energised in readiness for a new day. Good night.

Personal relationships

If you experience difficulty in mixing with other people, try to ask yourself why. Is it because you feel inferior to them; lack confidence in your own abilities; feel awkward and shy, or perhaps you have very little opportunity to meet and converse with people. Before starting this visualization, sit down and try to assess why you have a problem in this area.

Continuing to sit quietly, focus your concentration on yourself. How do you view yourself? Do you feel inferior and lack confidence? Look at your talents and interests. No matter how small these may be, they are still very important. A housewife is talented in the way she is able to run the home and care for a husband and family. The street sweeper has talents in the vital job that he is carrying out.

Likewise each one of us possesses talents but in order to work with them, we have first to acknowledge them.

Ask yourself how much you love you. If the answer is 'I don't', then start to. Each one of us is a unique, divine being, worthy of being able to give and receive love, but if we are unable to love ourselves, are we truly able to love anyone else?

Start loving yourself by looking in a mirror first thing in the morning and last thing at night and telling the image that you see, 'I love you, I love you, I love you'. This most probably sounds a crazy thing to do, but I can assure you that it works. As you grow to love this image, and therefore yourself, visualize yourself as a loving, talented being who has things to share with other people. Perhaps being able to help them in some way. Start by visualizing yourself mixing, talking, sharing and laughing with a small group of people. Visualize the topic of conversation and what you are able to contribute. See yourself being accepted and respected for what you are. Gradually increase the number of people present until you are able to visualize yourself mingling quite happily with a large crowd.

When you have perfected this, practise what you have learnt in a real life situation.

Making friends

Choosing a time when you will not be disturbed, sit down in your chosen place with a piece of paper and a pencil. Write down the kind of people whom you would like to meet. Include their sex, age, and a range of interests that you would like them to have. Also make a note of what you would expect these people to contribute to a friendship. At the same time, write down what you are prepared to give in forming and sustaining a friendship.

When you have completed this, place your pencil and paper on the floor and close your eyes. Visualize the people you have written about on your piece of paper. Visualize yourself meeting them in your chosen location and, in your imagination, formalise how you would start to create these new friendships. What you would say to them and what you would suggest doing. For example, would you invite them home for coffee, or suggest going out for a drink. Now visualize sharing interests and problems with your new friends and think of ways in which you could be a support and help to each other when needed. Remember that friendship must never be one-sided. It takes two people to make it in the same way that it takes two people to break it.

When you have completed this, think positively. Believe that the new friends who you have visualized will become a reality. If you do not believe, then nothing positive will happen.

Fear of the future

How easy it is to live in the past, anticipate or fear the future, but very rarely think of living in the present. The past, with all its pain, anguish, missed opportunities and mistakes, has gone. We can only look back and learn from its experiences. The future, with all of its fears and anticipations may never become a reality. This leaves us with the only true reality which is the present. How many times have you feared future events only to find that your fears were groundless? I believe that each of us has to learn to flow with the tide of life. To live in the 'now' and face the future when it comes. What a lot of energy is wasted through fear of unrealities. Having said this, I do appreciate that this philosophy is not easy but I also believe that it can be achieved with practice.

Sitting down in your chosen place, gently close your eyes and relax your body. Bring your concentration into the gentle inhalation and exhalation of the breath. With each exhalation, breathe out tension and fear; with each inhalation breathe in relaxation and joy.

When your mind and body have reached a state of peace and calm try to visualize what the future holds for you. Start by looking at the present state of your life. Ask yourself if you are achieving and doing what you would really like to do; if you are carrying out the mission that you came on earth for; if you feel that your life is being fulfilled and if you feel happy and content.

If not, ask yourself what would make you really happy, how you would like to spend the rest of your life, what your ambitions and aims of life are and how you could set about achieving these.

When you have done this, visualize yourself standing in the middle of a pathway. Behind you lies the shadow of how you have spent your life up to now. Ahead lies the path representing the rest of your life. This path, which has many turnings, is bathed in a gentle golden light. The turnings that lead off from the main path are named with the opportunities and challenges that life holds for you, should you choose to take them.

Slowly starting to walk down your path of life, look at the names displayed on the turnings that you pass. Perhaps some of them spell the things that you would really like to do but have not as yet been able to summon the courage to become involved in. Take a mental note of these so that you may give them further thought. When you have reached the end of the path, turn round and walk back to the place where you started, once more surveying the names of the turnings you pass. On reaching your starting point, sit down and try to feel within yourself which of the paths feels really right for you. Having done this, visualize yourself walking down your chosen path or paths. You may meet challenges and oppositions on the way, or it may demand a radical change in lifestyle, but if it is something that you really want to do you will find the strength to overcome all of these hurdles. One thing that you do need to be is positive. Visualize yourself fulfilling your ambitions and having the strength and courage to overcome whatever besets your path. Instead of feeling depressed and despondent about the future, visualize it as joy, fulfilment and happiness. Visualize yourself donning the armour of life and walking forward into the future with courage and strength.

The physical manifestations of stress

Any major changes in our lifestyle will make demands on our emotional and mental resources. Researchers have shown that as stresses accumulate for an individual, he or she becomes increasingly susceptible to physical illness, mental and emotional problems and even accidental injuries. The parts of the body most susceptible and the diseases which manifest are:

- **The brain** Many mental and emotional problems, among them anxiety, depression and schizophrenia, may be precipitated by stress.
- **The hair** Some forms of baldness, among them alopecia areata, are linked to high levels of stress.
- **The mouth** Mouth problems, such as mouth ulcers and lichen planus, frequently occur when a person is under stress.

- **The lungs** Asthmatics often find that their condition worsens when they are subjected to high levels of stress.
- **The heart** Attacks of angina and disturbances of heart rate and rhythm often occur at the same time as, or follow closely upon, a period of stress.
- **The digestive tract** Diseases of the digestive tract, which may be either caused or exacerbated by stress, include gastritis, stomach and duodenal ulcers, ulcerative colitis and irritable bowel syndrome.
- **The reproductive organs** Stress-related problems in this part of the body include amenorrhoea in women and impotence and premature ejaculation in men.
- **The bladder** The bladders of many women and men react to stress by being 'irritable'.
- **The muscles** The muscles become tense and various minor muscular twitches and 'nervous tics' become more noticeable when a person is under stress. Also, the muscular tremor of Parkinson's disease is more marked at such times.
- **The skin** Outbreaks of eczema and psoriasis can be attributed to abnormal stress.

If you are suffering from any of the above conditions, it is advisable to seek medical advice and not just assume that the condition is the result of stress. If you are suffering from a stress-related condition, then it is advisable to evaluate your life in order to try and eliminate some, if not all, of the causes. All of the conditions mentioned above can be treated with drugs. Unfortunately, these will only alleviate the symptoms. If the cause is not dealt with, symptoms will reoccur somewhere else in the body.

—————— Evaluating your life ——————

This can be a very difficult and sometimes traumatic experience. Frequently, we have no wish to face the cause of a problem because its solution proves to be too difficult or painful. I do know from personal experience that if the cause is suppressed, it will continue to confront us until we have the courage to do something about it. I have frequently heard people say that they are unable to deal with their stress because in so doing, it would involve hurting another person. Perhaps the pain that the other person suffers is part of their growth and understanding. In holding back, not only do we make ourselves ill but we could be denying the other person an opportunity for growth and awareness. I believe that we should surround all people involved in the elimination of our stress problem with love and protection and visualize them growing in wisdom and understanding.

In order to help you assess your present stress level, given below are 21 questions. If you score over 160, your stress level is high and could result in ill health. Between 80 and 160 rates less chance of ill health but indicates that you still are in need of reducing your stress level. Between 50 and 80; be aware of your lifestyle. Under 50, there is little chance of you being affected physically.

Stress Evaluation

1 Has your partner died recently? **25 points**	2 Have you recently undergone divorce? **20 points**	3 Have you separated from your partner? **20 points**
4 Has a close member of your family recently died? **15 points**	5 Have you recently undergone hospitalisation? **13 points**	6 Have you married recently or effected a reconciliation with your partner? **13 points**
7 Have you recently become pregnant? **12 points**	8 Have you recently been made redundant? **12 points**	9 Are there health problems related to a close member of your family? **10 points**
10 Have you recently retired? **10 points**	11 Has a close friend died recently? **9 points**	12 Have you changed your job? **9 points**

13 Are you facing financial difficulties? **9 points**	14 Are you under pressure from in-laws? **8 points**	15 Are you caring for an aged parent? **8 points**
16 Are you under pressure of work? **8 points**	17 Have you recently taken on a substantial debt or mortgage? **7 points**	18 Are any of your children leaving home? **6 points**
19 Do you suffer from pre-menstrual tension? **5 points**	20 Do you travel a lot in your job? **4 points**	21 Have you altered your diet recently? **3 points**

If, after completing this evaluation, you have scored over 80, then may I suggest that you start working with the following visualization and the other visualization techniques given in this book.

Making changes

Sitting quietly in your chosen place, when you have relaxed your body and mind, start to look back over the present day. Try to recall any stressful situations. Having done this, take your mind back over the past week; then the past month and finally the past year. Ask yourself if the stress that you are experiencing has lasted for this duration of time or even longer. If the answer is longer, try to recall when it first started. Try to evaluate the cause, no matter how painful this may be. Try to answer truthfully what you feel to be the right and best solution to this. Now try to visualize how you will set this solution into practice. In your visualization, 'see' all those who may be involved surrounded by love and visualize them learning and growing from your decisions.

Practise this every day, visualizing every detail of the changes that you wish to make in your life. By doing this, you should find the courage and strength to carry through what you intuitively know to be the right thing.

As I have already explained earlier in this chapter, one of the effects of stress is tension. To work with this we need to learn how to relax. For a lot of people, tension is the norm. What we now have to do is to reverse this and make relaxation the norm. The following chapter deals with relaxation and the various techniques and visualizations that can be practised to aid relaxation.

4

RELAXATION

In the last chapter, we ascertained that tension is a tightness or squeezing that occurs in the organism mentally, emotionally and physically. If we squeeze ourselves mentally, we induce a headache; when we get 'uptight', emotionally we feel uneasy and if we tense ourselves physically we bring about a multitude of aches and pains. These actions needlessly use a lot of energy and occur in a vast amount of the population each day.

If for you tension has become the norm, you have most probably forgotten not only how to relax, but what the state of relaxation is and feels like. In order to distinguish between these two states, try the following exercise.

Relaxation technique

1 Lie down in your chosen place as described in chapter 1.
2 When your body is comfortable and your mind relaxed, bring your awareness into both of your feet. Tense up all the muscles in your feet; hold for a few seconds and then let go. Feel your feet becoming relaxed.
3 From your feet, move your awareness into both of your legs, from your ankles to the tops of your thighs. Tense the muscles in your legs; hold for a few seconds before letting go, allowing the muscles in your legs to relax.
4 From your legs, bring your awareness into your abdomen. Tense not only the muscles that surround the pelvic girdle but also the organs that are contained within the abdominal cavity. Be aware of how uncomfortable this feels. Hold and then relax.

5 From your abdomen concentrate on your solar plexus, the muscles that form this part of the body and the organs, such as the stomach, pancreas and liver, which are housed here. Tense these muscles and organs; take note of how you feel when you do this; hold and then relax.

6 Now bring your awareness into your chest. Tense the muscles that surround your ribcage and the organs contained within the chest cavity. Be conscious of how this affects your breathing and your heartbeat. Hold and relax.

7 Move your concentration from your chest to your shoulders, arms and hands. Tense all of the muscles in this part of your body. Note the pressure that this puts upon your neck and head. Hold and relax.

8 Lastly, concentrate on your head and neck. Tense the muscles in this part of your body, screwing up your face, eyes, jaws and tongue. Take note of how this action affects your shoulders by raising them and see how easy it is for this kind of tension to cause headaches. Hold and relax.

9 Finally, tense the whole of your body; every muscle and organ. Ask yourself how this feels and how you think it affects you not only physically, but also emotionally and mentally. Hold and then relax for ten to fifteen minutes before continuing with your normal daily routine.

To discover how tense you have become during the course of a day, periodically stop what you are doing, stand perfectly still and mentally scan your body from your feet to your head. Take note of all the places that are tense. Having done this, remedy the situation by letting go and relaxing. Doing this on a regular basis will help you to start living a relaxed, instead of a tense, life.

—— The importance of relaxation ——

If squeezing and contracting results in tension, then the relief of this condition would result from letting go and relaxing. Unfortunately, most of us think of relaxation as something that is done only at specific times. These times are normally in the evening on returning from work or school or when the normal household chores have been completed.

Most people's idea of relaxation is sitting in front of the television; reading the newspaper; taking alcoholic beverage which helps to induce sleep. Unfortunately, none of these pastimes will bring about true relaxation. To relax completely, we must relax mentally and emotionally. Television may help us to 'switch off' from problems and anxieties but it still acts as a mental stimulant and creates noise pollution. Alcohol will gradually dull the reactions of the brain and nerves and act as a tranquillizer or relaxant but, if used excessively, it will damage the liver.

The fear of silence

Unfortunately, with the present pace of life and the continual surrounding noise, the art of silence has been lost. For many, spending time in silence can be frightening. They feel lost, lonely and unable to handle the thoughts that continuously bombard their minds. They are unable to be alone with themselves; they hurriedly switch on the radio, play music or find companionship with other human beings. In order to learn the art of relaxation, we have again to recapture that art of silence and learn to be alone and content with ourselves.

Visualizations for silence

One way to start practising is to spend a set time each day alone, without external noise. At first, this may feel very strange and 'unnatural'. If you experience fear, try to find the reason why. Take this opportunity to start looking in on yourself; how you feel and what thoughts are coming to mind. If you find yourself thinking negatively, try to change to positive thoughts. After a while, silence should become to you a necessity and not just an exercise; something that you welcome and look forward to.

The following visualizations will help you to appreciate a state of silence.

The cave

Go to your chosen place or to a place that is devoid of noise. Either lie down, sit on a chair or on the floor, whichever you find most comfortable.

Quieten your mind by releasing the continual stream of thoughts passing through it; then relax your body. When all is quiet and still, try to be aware of the silence that surrounds you. Listen to any small noise that may be present, trying to shut it out of your consciousness. Try to listen to the noise of your own breathing and the sound of your heart.

When you feel relaxed and still, visualize yourself in mountainous terrain. Gazing up at the vast rock formations that surround you fills you with awe and wonder. Their height, strength and might makes you feel very small as you view them from the beginning of a gentle undulating path which winds its way up to the peak of one of the smaller mountains. Looking up at the mountain, you observe that the lower part is formed mainly by grass-covered slopes. These gradually change to stark rock formations with flowers and grasses appearing in the crevices.

Relaxed and warmed by the sun, you start your journey along the path. As you ascend the mountain you pass sheep, and encounter streams spiralling their way to the earth. In places, the path becomes steep, making you stop to rest awhile and enabling you to drink in the beauty of the panoramic scene before you.

Leaving the gently undulating slopes, your path starts to take you through and over rock formations. You find this necessitates climbing or scrambling over the occasional boulder.

Gradually the path along which you are walking passes alongside a sheer rock face. Stopping to look at how this has been formed, you notice an opening to the right of where you are standing. The opening is not very high and you have to go down on your hands and knees in order to look inside. It appears to lead to a small cave, but, as yet, your eyes have not grown accustomed to the darkness. Even though you feel slightly scared, you decide to explore further.

Crawling through the opening, you enter a small cave. Because your eyes have not yet adjusted to the small amount of light, you are only able to explore your surroundings by feeling with your hands. The rock which forms the sides and floor of the cave is smooth and cold. There are several small boulders scattered on the floor. All is very still and silent.

Gradually the inside of the cave comes into vision. It is higher than you anticipated, enabling you to stand upright. Walking to one of the boulders at the back of the cave, you sit down and rest awhile. Through the opening you can see the play of sunlight creating moving, dancing shadows on distant mountains.

Closing your eyes, you become aware of the silence that surrounds you. Allow this silence to permeate every part of your being. Try to go into yourself, exploring your feelings and thoughts. Visualize your fears and your problems dissolving to reveal that beautiful Divine being which is your true self. Visualize a pale golden light flooding the cave and forming an orb of protection around you.

When you feel ready to leave, stand up and walk to the mouth of the cave. Going down on your hands and knees, crawl through the opening and back to the place where you started your visualization.

Bring your concentration to your physical body. Start to increase your inhalation and exhalation. Then, when you are ready, open your eyes.

The dolphin

Go to your chosen place and either lie or sit on the floor or sit on a chair. Make sure that your body is relaxed and comfortable then gently close your eyes.

Imagine yourself standing on a beach in the Caribbean. It is a very hot, sunny day and the only shade to be found is beneath the palm trees and the numerous coloured sunshades adorning the beach. Many exotic, brightly coloured birds fly overhead; their cries mingle with the sound of the waves as they break on the sea shore.

Dressed in a swimsuit, take yourself down to the edge of the sea. The coolness of the waves as they break over your feet and legs feels wonderful compared with the heat of the day.

Wading out into the water until it reaches your waist, you allow the sea to lift you gently, empowering you to swim in its cool refreshing water. Turning and floating on your back enables you to look up into the clear blue sky. A great sense of peace and serenity floods through you.

As you float along, caressed by the gentle waves, you feel something nudge your side. Turning your head, you see a large grey form swimming beneath you. It turns and swims back to you. As it approaches it lifts its head from the water and you find yourself looking into the face of a dolphin. It swims around you encouraging play. In comparison with its size and weight, it plays very gently and makes you laugh at some of its antics. As you begin to lose your fear, you become conscious that it is trying to communicate with you telepathically. It is encouraging you to hold its fin because it wants to show you the beautiful undersea world in which it lives. It tells you to have no fear of drowning because it will show you how to breathe normally beneath the water.

Holding the dolphin's fin, it takes you down into the beauty and wonder that lies beneath the water. You pass fish of all shapes, sizes and colours; sea plants and rocks and beautiful banks of coral. When you reach the ocean bed, the dolphin nudges you to sit beside it. With your hand resting on its back, you watch sea urchins appear and scuttle across the sandy floor. All is silent as you watch the never ending movement of the creatures that live in this watery world.

Turning and looking into the dolphin's eyes, you are able to see a reflection of yourself. One by one your tensions, stresses, problems, aches and pains are taken away to be dissolved in the water. In the silence, you are able to see your life unfolding before you; you are shown the gifts that you have been given and how these can be used. You see the various paths that are open to you, and which of these will bring you contentment and satisfaction. You also learn that it is only in the silence that we are able to communicate with our higher, true self. That Divine part of us which knows the answers to our problems, knows the path we should tread and wants to communicate with us, if only we will listen.

Feeling a slight movement from the dolphin, you know that it is time to return to your own land environment. Taking hold once more of the dolphin's fin, you are gently propelled through the water. As your head breaks the surface, you find yourself back in the room where you started.

As you slowly start to increase your inhalation and exhalation, you can still see the dolphin in your mind's eye and he assures you that whenever you wish to repeat the journey, he will be waiting. Waiting to take you into the silence that can be found beneath the water.

Exercises and visualizations for relaxation

Prior to practising relaxation visualizations, it can be beneficial to perform simple stretching movements. The act of stretching the body helps to start releasing tension from the muscles. If you have been sitting still for a long period of time, experience how good it feels to stand up and stretch. The same applies when first getting out of bed in the morning.

The following sections give a selection of basic movements to practise prior to relaxation. Each movement should be performed slowly, gently and with full awareness on the muscles that are being used. Try to ascertain the degree of stiffness in your body and notice how this gradually eases with practice.

The first movement (illustrated below, left) is learning to stand correctly before stretching the whole body (below, right).

Standing correctly

1 Stand on the floor with your feet about two inches apart. Make sure that both feet are parallel, your big toes in line with each other and your weight distributed evenly on both feet. Place your hands by your sides. Start to 'lift' your body from your feet, tuck in your tailbone, lift your spine, drop and take back your shoulders in order to open out your chest, extend your neck, allowing your head to remain free and mobile.

2 Breathing in, stretch your arms up over your head until the palms of your hands are joined and your arms are brought as close as you can get them to your ears. Breathing out, bring your arms back down to your sides.

3 On the next inhalation, raise your arms as before, visualizing any tension as a grey mist which you breathe out of your body on the exhalation. Repeat five times.

When you have become familiar with this exercise, try performing it lying on the floor instead of standing.

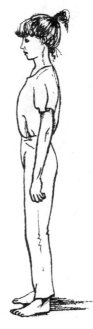

Figure 1

Chest expansion

1 Stand on the floor with your feet slightly apart and your big toes in line with each other. Make sure that your spine is straight and allow your arms to be relaxed by your sides. Take your shoulders down and back in order to open out the chest. (Figure 1)

2 Take your arms behind your back and clasp your hands. (Figure 2) Keeping your body in an upright position, raise your arms behind you as far as possible. Feel the expansion that this gives to your chest and the release of tension from your shoulders and arms. (Figure 3)

3 With your arms still raised behind you, gently start to bend forward from the waist as far as is possible without strain. Hold for a count of five. (Figure 4)

4 Raise your body and gently bend backward from your waist. Hold for a count of five before releasing your arms and relaxing. (Figure 5)

Figure 2

Figure 3

Figure 4

Figure 5

Next time you perform this movement, visualize your spine as a string of flower buds. Each vertebra represents one bud. As you work with the spine in this exercise, imagine the buds springing open to show beautiful golden flowers of light. Visualize each petal of each flower radiating a golden light which travels along the nerves connected to the individual vertebra and through to the organs and muscles of the body.

Side bend

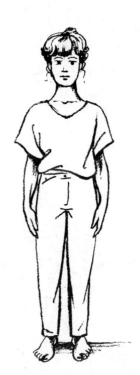

1 Stand erect with your feet about four inches apart. Make sure that your feet are parallel to each other with the big toes in line. (Figure 1)
2 Raise your arms to shoulder level with the palms of the hands facing down. (Figure 2) Keeping your knees locked, slowly bend from your waist over to the left side. Attempt to touch your left knee or thigh with your left hand. (Figure 3) Straighten the body and then bend over to your right side, attempting to touch your right knee or thigh with your right hand (Figures 4 and 5). Straighten the body and relax.

Figure 1

When you next perform this movement, visualize your sides as elastic. As you bend, feel the elastic being gently stretched. At first, this may prove difficult because the elastic is hard and stiff. But, with practice, the elastic becomes softer and easier to manipulate.

Figure 2   **Figure 3**

Figure 4   **Figure 5**

The cat

1 Kneel on all fours. Your knees should be slightly apart, your hands placed in line with your knees and beneath your shoulders.
2 Keeping your arms straight and bringing your awareness into your spine, slowly breathe out. As you exhale, arch your spine, making it as round as possible; contract your stomach muscles towards your spine; allow your chin to move towards your chest bone.
3 Breathing in and keeping your arms straight, hollow your spine, so that your stomach drops towards the floor; take your shoulders back and lift your head.
4 Continue to work with this in a smooth, slow and continuous movement. Centre your mind on your spine. As you move the spine with each inhalation and exhalation, try to visualize the separate movement of each vertebra. If you are working too quickly, this will be impossible. If you find your mind wandering, gently bring it back to the task in hand. If we are able to keep our spine supple, the whole of the body will be rejuvenated.

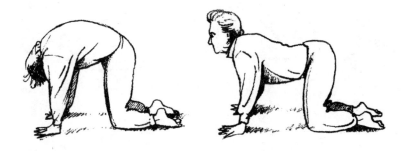

To strengthen the back and abdominal muscles

1 Sit on the floor with your legs stretched in front of you and your hands placed on your thighs. Very slowly, lower your back to the floor and raise your arms over your head. Stretch the whole body.

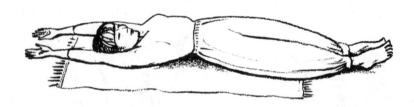

2 Bring your hands down to your sides with the palms touching the floor. Bend your knees over your abdomen and then straighten them. Keeping your legs straight, lower them to the floor as slowly as possible. Feel this movement working on your abdominal muscles.

3 When your legs have reached the floor, place your hands on your thighs and slowly raise your trunk back to a sitting position. If, initially, you find this difficult then use your hands to help you.

4 From the sitting position, slowly bend forward, sliding your hands down your legs to your feet. When you have reached your maximum position, come back to the sitting position and relax.

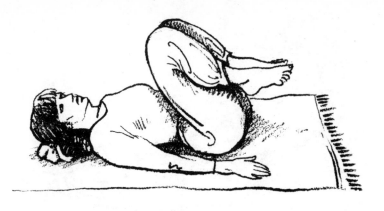

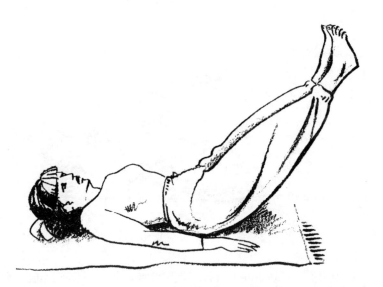

Start by repeating this exercise two to three times. As your body becomes stronger and more supple, increase the number of repetitions. Visualize your body moving through this exercise with grace and precision. Remember that the body is the temple of the soul, therefore we should endeavour to keep it healthy, strong and beautiful.

When you have become familiar with the movements, imagine that you are a puppet with strings attached to your feet, hands, shoulders and head. As you perform each movement, visualize your strings being pulled by an unseen force, enabling your body to execute the movements correctly and effortlessly.

Having completed these movements, lie down in your chosen place for relaxation. Choose one of the visualization relaxations given below. You may find it beneficial to record these on cassette in order that you can play them while relaxing.

The sea

Prepare yourself for this relaxation as described in chapter 1. Make sure that your body is warm and comfortable and that your mind is at peace.

Imagine that it is a beautifully warm and sunny day and that you are lying on the beach in a small sandy cove, surrounded by grey cliffs that have small green rock plants growing out of their crevices. You feel the softness of the sand beneath you and its slight movement as some of the small grains trickle through your fingers. Look at the blue sky above and sense the warmth from the sun penetrating your body. Close your eyes and listen to the cry of the seagulls and the roar of the waves as they break on the shore.

Lying and listening to these sounds, you become aware of the waves breaking on the shore and the sea travelling across the beach until it very gently laps over your feet. Initially the water feels cold in comparison with the warmth of the sun. As the water recedes, you feel it draw out and take with it any tension that has accumulated in your feet. Your feet relax and feel heavy. The next wave breaks and gently rolls over the sand, covering your feet and legs. The coldness of the water feels invigorating. It recedes and takes your tension with it. Your legs relax. Hearing the next wave coming and breaking on the shore, you wait for the water to touch your feet and then move over your legs, hands, lower part of your arms and abdomen. The muscles and organs in your abdomen contract slightly as they experience the coldness of the sea. The water recedes and you allow it to take your tension with it. Listening, and waiting expectantly, you prepare yourself for the next wave. It comes and covers your body up to your neck. A slight shiver goes through your body as the water comes into contact with your chest. But this is compensated by the feeling of lightness and relaxation that you experience when the water has drawn out and taken with it all of your tension.

You know that the next wave will cover your entire body, but you are not afraid. Your intuition tells you that you will be able to breathe normally under this water. Wait and listen. It is coming. You embrace the water as it covers you and you give to it all your tension, toxins and pain with gratitude and love. The water slowly recedes. It leaves you feeling completely relaxed and renewed, physically, mentally and spiritually. A feeling of joy pervades you as you once more become aware of the warmth of the sun revitalising and re-energising the whole of your being.

Lie in this state for as long as you feel comfortable before bringing your body back into everyday activity as described in chapter 1.

Magnolia blossom

Prepare yourself for relaxation as described in chapter 1. When your body is warm and comfortable and your mind at peace, imagine yourself standing at the top of a winding flight of twelve stairs. The stairs are carpeted in blue and the wall on either side is painted a very pale grey. As you descend each stair, your body will enter a deeper state of relaxaton.

Walking down the first step, your body starts to feel relaxed and at peace. The second and third steps make you feel heavier and per-mits the release of tension. As you descend the stairs repeat to yourself: 'My body is becoming heavier; I feel warm, relaxed and at peace'. Continuing to walk down the fourth and fifth steps, allow your body to become so heavy that it feels as though it is sinking into the floor. Again repeat to yourself: 'My body is sinking into a deeper state of relaxation; I feel warm, relaxed and at peace'. Transcending the sixth and seventh steps, your body becomes so relaxed and heavy that you would find it difficult to move, unless it was really necessary. Repeat to yourself: 'My body is very relaxed and heavy; I feel warm and at peace'. On descending the eighth and ninth steps, you are able to see a door at the bottom of the stairs. As your body starts to enter a state of total peace and relaxation, repeat to yourself: 'I am totally relaxed, warm, well and happy'. Descending the final three stairs, you find yourself standing in front of the door. It is oval at the top, made of wood with a wooden han-dle on the right-hand side. Turn the handle and push the door open.

Stepping through the door, you find yourself in the countryside. It is a warm spring day and the trees are decked in their pale spring foliage. In front of you stands a pale magenta magnolia tree in full blossom. Walking over to this tree you sit down beneath its branches. Gazing up into its branches, the blossom appears as giant bells.

The warmth of the sun and the peace of the countryside makes you drowsy and as you drift into sleep you find yourself lying inside the magnolia blossom. The petals are soft and their delicate perfume surrounds you with an aura of peace. The pale magenta colour allows you to let go of any remaining tension and fills you with a deep spiritual love.

When you feel that the time is right for you to return to everyday activity, allow yourself to emerge from the magnolia flower. Stand up and walk back towards the wooden door. Walk through the door, closing it behind you. As you start to climb back up the stairs, feel yourself gently emerging from your deep state of relaxation. On reaching the top step, become aware of your physical body lying on the floor. Fully emerge from your relaxation as described in chapter 1.

The crystal

Prepare yourself for relaxation as described in chapter 1.

Lying in your chosen place, imagine that you are holding a large quartz crystal in your hands. Take note of its hexagonal shape and the various patterns that have formed inside the crystal. Try to feel the energy emanating from it, remembering that it is a living entity.

Looking round the crystal, you find a door embedded in one of its six sides. As you survey the door, the crystal starts to grow until it is large enough for you to enter.

Walking through the opening, you find yourself in a hexagonal room. In the centre is a couch and a table. On the table is a pencil, paper and a crystal box. You are invited to lie down on the couch with the pencil and paper.

As you lie in the crystal room, you are surrounded by rainbows formed by the refraction of light through the crystal. Relaxing in the peaceful energy surrounding you, you are invited to write down any problems, anxieties or uncertainties that prevent your total enjoyment of life. When you have completed this, go to the crystal box, open the lid and place what you have written inside.

Lying back on the couch, a bright angelic being emerges from the crystal box and stands in front of you. Looking into this being's eyes, you see written the answers to your problems and anxieties. You are made to realise that these are your challenges in life – the hurdles over which you must go in order to grow and evolve along life's path. You are invited to lay down the burdens which do not belong to you in order that your journey may be made lighter. When you have done this, they are blessed and placed into the crystal box. The angelic being, which is your higher self, then blesses you and bestows upon you the peace and relaxation which passeth all man's understanding before vanishing from sight.

Carrying the gifts that you have been given, stand up and walk back through the door of the crystal. As you do this, you find yourself lying on the floor contemplating the crystal in your hands. Thank the crystal for what it has revealed to you.

When you are ready, bring yourself out of this state of relaxation as described in chapter 1.

5

SELF-HEALING

Unlike a piece of man-made machinery, our body is a beautiful instrument which, given the right conditions, is self-healing. In order to procure the right conditions, we have to appreciate the workings of the physical body and the aura which surrounds and interpenetrates it. Having acquired this knowledge, we can then start working with it. Repeating what is written in the introduction, bringing about the right conditions frequently requires change. This can be both difficult and painful. But, if we wish to grow and evolve as human beings, we have to have the courage to walk through the dark tunnels of life in order to appreciate the light.

The aura

The aura or electromagnetic field that surrounds and interpenetrates with the human body is ovoid in shape. The widest part is around the head and the narrowest beneath the feet. It comprises seven layers, each layer slightly larger than its predecessor.

The seven layers constitute the physical body; the etheric sheath or energy body; the astral sheath or emotional body; the mental body; the higher mental; the causal and the bodyless body.

The bodyless body establishes that Divine part of us which has no beginning and no ending; which through practices such as meditation, enables us to realise and become one with it. From the moment of birth we are subject to conditioning. Through this, we forget our life's purpose. We then become like travellers working our way across a strange country without a map. Apart from conditioning, we are also given free will. This enables us to choose which path we take. Unfortunately, we do not always choose the correct one. How many times can you remember sitting at one of life's crossroads. Intuitively you know which way you should travel but insight reveals it to be a very stony and difficult path, so you take what looks to be the easier way. This may prove to be correct for a time but gradually you will be brought back by your higher self to the path which you intuitively felt to be correct. Our true self knows its chosen way and will, at all costs, continually confront us with it until we find the courage to take it.

The higher mental body could be called the voice of our intuition. If we learn to 'tune in' to this part of our self, we are able to receive Divine inspiration. The answers to life's problems will be revealed and we will be taught spiritual truths and cosmic law. The law which all creation adheres to and works with.

The mental body is connected with thought. Each thought that we think creates a pattern or form. These accumulate in the mental body and can be projected out into the environment, surrounding us with thought forms which we and other individuals have created.

These thought forms also attract the thought forms surrounding us that are of a similar nature. Therefore, if we think negative thoughts we will attract negative thought forms; likewise, positive thoughts attract positive thought forms. It is therefore important to have a positive outlook on life, especially when working with self-healing.

When working with absent healing, the mental body is part of the aura with which we work. We visualize the person who has requested healing lying in peaceful surroundings. We then create beautiful healing forms and project them to the patient. The greater the control we have over the mental body, the greater the strength of healing. When we have acquired the power of thought, it must only be used for the good of others. Remember the law of karma; whatever good you do will be repaid with good; whatever evil, retribution will follow.

The emotional or astral sheath is our 'feeling' body. In those people who have not learnt to be the master over their emotions, this body is in a state of imbalance. Because it is interspersed with the other layers of the aura and the physical body, these too are affected. It is similar to one of the organs of the physical body being diseased and the rest of the body being affected through trying to compensate for it.

The sheath nearest to the physical body is the etheric. The etheric and physical body are closely interwoven and disintegrate together at death. Every physical particle has its etheric counterpart, which is a perfect replica of the physical form. This is why it is known as the etheric double, and why people who have had a limb amputated can still feel pain or sensation from it – it is still present in its etheric form. The etheric lays down the basic pattern upon which the physical body is built. This means that the resilience of the physical body is directly related to the tone and quality of the etheric body. Apart from containing the nadis, already described in chapter 2, it contains seven major, and 21 minor, chakras plus numerous acupuncture points. A major chakra is defined by the crossing of 21 energy lines; a minor chakra constitutes 14 energy lines, and an acupuncture point seven.

The chakras

The seven major chakras are situated along the etheric spine. These force centres can be found in each of the six layers constituting the aura, but their primary importance is at the etheric level. They are both the transformers and the transmitters of energy for each of the layers. In appearance they resemble a wheel, the Sanskrit word 'chakra' meaning a wheel or circle. The energies rhythmically pulsate and circulate through the core of this wheel. These centres are never still, but the speed with which they rotate depends to some extent upon the state of health of the individual.

Five of the major chakras in the etheric body are in alignment with the spine, while the sixth and seventh are located between the eyebrows, and just above the crown of the head, respectively. The size of these centres is related to an individual's personal development. In an under-developed person the chakras will be small in size, slow in movement and dull in colour. In a more intelligent and sensitive person, they will be larger in size, faster in movement, and brighter in colour.

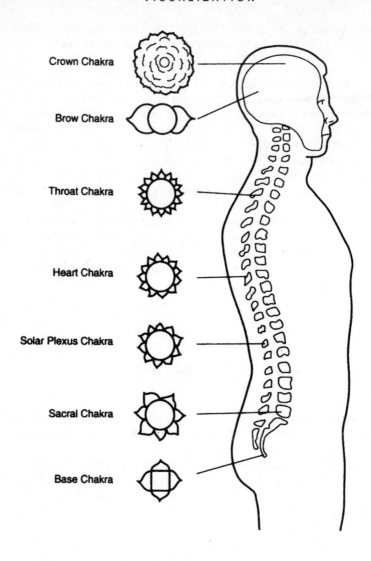

The position of the chakras on the spine

To each of these chakras is ascribed a dominant colour, and each has a special link with one of the endocrine glands and with physical organs. In order to understand the importance of the correct functioning of these centres, let us look at them individually.

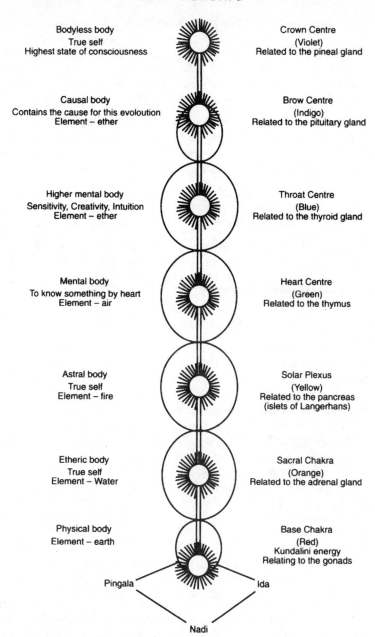

| Bodyless body
True self
Highest state of consciousness | | Crown Centre
(Violet)
Related to the pineal gland |

Causal body
Contains the cause for this evoloution
Element – ether

Brow Centre
(Indigo)
Related to the pituitary gland

Higher mental body
Sensitivity, Creativity, Intuition
Element – ether

Throat Centre
(Blue)
Related to the thyroid gland

Mental body
To know something by heart
Element – air

Heart Centre
(Green)
Related to the thymus

Astral body
True self
Element – fire

Solar Plexus
(Yellow)
Related to the pancreas
(islets of Langerhans)

Etheric body
True self
Element – Water

Sacral Chakra
(Orange)
Related to the adrenal gland

Physical body
Element – earth

Base Chakra
(Red)
Kundalini energy
Relating to the gonads

Pingala   Ida

Nadi

Information related to the chakras

The base chakra

The base chakra is situated at the end of the coccyx. Its dominant colour is red. It is associated with the earth, the physical body and is the centre of physical energy and vitality. It regulates the sense of smell, is associated with will and power, and is ascribed to the planet Mars.

The parts of the body affected by this chakra are the legs, feet, bones, large intestine, spine and nervous system. The endocrine glands to which it is related are the gonads. These constitute the testes in the male, and the ovaries in the female.

The hormones secreted from the testes are called androgens, the most important being testosterone, which is responsible for the changes which take place in a male during puberty.

Apart from producing ova, the ovaries secrete oestrogen and proge-strone. The secretion of oestrogen is influenced by the follicle stimu-lating hormone (FSH) which is produced by the pituitary gland. Oestrogen helps to regulate the menstrual cycle and develops the sex-ual characteristics of the female. Progesterone sensitises the mucous membrane of the uterus in preparation for the fertilised ovum.

When this centre is functioning fully, it gives a person a strong will to live on the physical plane. He/she is filled with vitality and energy, nothing is too much trouble, and the whole of life becomes an adven-ture. If, however, this centre is blocked, the person's energy levels will be low, they will have no enthusiasm for life, and will feel unable to carry out their daily work. They may also experience sexual, fertil-ity or menstrual difficulties or problems with any of the parts of the body which are governed by this chakra. People who have the gift of auric sight are able to ascertain if a chakra is balanced by the colour and degree of colour radiating from it, also by the presence of grey patches over and around the centre and by its speed of rotation. People who are frigid or who have been conditioned that sex is dirty and should not be discussed, or who have been sexually abused as a child or young adult, frequently have problems with this centre. Likewise those who, through the practice of various meditation tech-niques have become 'unearthed', have become so heavenly minded that they no longer have their feet on the ground.

People suffering from disease in areas of the body connected with one or more of the chakras will find it beneficial to work with the visualization techniques ascribed to the chakras. Also, under the chapter on 'mandalas', geometric forms are given for each chakra for the reader to colour. This again has proven to be a great help in balancing the individual centres.

Visualization with the base chakra

Sit down either on a chair or on the floor, in your chosen place. Relax your body, making sure that your spine is straight.

Bring your concentration to the base of your spine, the coccyx. Visualize a disc of red pulsating energy. Try to feel this energy. In so doing, you may experience heat, cold, pain or a tingling sensation at the base of your spine.

On your next inhalation, breathe in through the earth, a shaft of pure red light. Visualize this colour becoming concentrated in the base chakra; then, as you breathe out, visualize the rotation of the chakra fanning this clear, bright colour down your legs to your feet; through your large intestine; your nervous system and to your ovaries, if you are a female, and testes if you are a male. Watching this colour circulate through the parts of the body affected by this chakra, allow your body to be energised and earthed to this planet. Feel a warm glow spread through your lower body. Continue to work with this visualization and the ones that follow for as long as you feel is necessary. When you are ready, resume normal breathing, become aware of your physical body, and gently open your eyes.

If you are suffering from infertility, work mainly with this colour on the ovaries or testes. Visualize them functioning to their full potential.

———— The sacral chakra ————

The sacral chakra is situated halfway between the pubis and the navel. The dominant colour which radiates from it is orange. It is associated with the etheric sheath, the element water, and affects the flow of fluids in the body.

This centre links with the emotions of fear and anxiety. The glands and organs that it influences are the skin, the female reproductive organs, the kidneys, bladder, circulatory system and lymphatic system. The endocrine glands associated with it are the adrenals.

— 65 —

The adrenal glands are situated one on the top of each kidney. They are approximately one inch in length and yellowish in colour. They constitute an outer cortex and an interior or medulla. The hormones secreted by the cortex are influenced by the hormone adrenocorticotrophin (ACTH) which is secreted by the pituitary gland.

The cortex is responsible for secreting a number of hormones known as corticosteroids. These are divided into three main groups. The first group is the mineral corticoids. These work on the tubules of the kidneys, helping to retain sodium and chloride in the body, maintaining blood pressure and aiding in the excretion of excess potassium.

The second group is called gluco-corticoids, the most important being hydrocortisone (cortisol). These assist in the conversion of carbohydrates into glycogen. They increase the blood sugar, help in the utilisation of fat, decrease the number of lymphocytes and eosinophils in the blood, and reduce the rate at which certain connective tissue cells multiply. In excess this action tends to suppress natural healing and therefore delays it.

The third group is similar to the hormones produced by the gonads. They influence the growth and sex development in both male and female.

The medulla of the adrenal glands secretes adrenalin and noradrenalin. Adrenalin stimulates the sympathetic nervous system and causes the arteries of the body to constrict, resulting in an increase in the heartbeat and a rise in blood pressure. Adrenalin also stimulates the liver into converting glycogen into glucose which it then pours into the bloodstream.

When this centre is blocked, it can result in a woman being unable to reach orgasm during sexual union. In a male, it manifests as premature ejaculation or the inability to achieve an erection. Other disorders that can be caused are abnormalities in the kidney and bladder functions, such as infections and poor urinary control, and problems with the circulatory system, menstruation and production of seminal fluids.

When this centre is functioning to its full potential, it opens the intuitive powers. When it first awakens, it can upset the sexual energies and heighten awareness to external stimuli. These will again find their own balance but on a higher level of consciousness.

Visualization with the sacral chakra

Go to your chosen place and sit either on the floor or on a chair. Gently start to relax your body, making sure that your spine is straight.

Bring your awareness to the point halfway between your pubis and navel. Visualize the sacral energy chakra which is found here as a deep orange chrysanthemum. On the next in breath, still keeping your attention focused, visualize a shaft of deep orange light coming through the earth and into this chakra. As the colour comes into contact with the chrysanthemum, watch the petals start to radiate a deep, clear, orange light. Slowly breathing out, watch how the orange light reflects from the petals into your abdomen. Through the continuation of visualizing the inhalation and exhalation of this bright, clear, orange, the sacral chakra becomes clear of blockages and comes into balance. The clear orange rays bring health and harmony to your adrenal glands, kidneys, uterus, ovaries, bladder and circulatory system. Concentrating on this centre enables you to look at the cause of any blockages and disharmony centered in and around your abdomen. Looking at and recognising the cause is the first step to removing it.

When you are ready, bring your awareness back to your physical body. Deepen your inhalation and exhalation and when you feel ready gently open your eyes.

—— The solar plexus chakra ——

The solar plexus chakra is situated between the twelfth thoracic and the first lumbar vertebra. Its dominant colour is yellow and it is associated with the astral or emotional sheath.

This is the centre of vitality in the physical body because it is where prana (the upward-moving vitality) and apana (the downward-moving vitality) meet, generating the heat that is necessary to support life. When these two energies join, the centre awakens.

This centre is chiefly concerned with the process of digestion and absorption. The processes and organs influenced by it are the breath, the diaphragm, the stomach, duodenum, gall-bladder and liver. The endocrine gland with which it is associated is the pancreas.

The pancreas is situated behind the stomach, and lies transversely across the posterior abdominal wall at the level of the first and second lumbar vertebrae. This gland is similar in structure to the salivary glands that are found in the mouth.

Only part of the pancreas is endocrine. These are the 'islets of langerhans' which secrete insulin, which is responsible for the metabolism of sugar. Without insulin, the muscles would be unable to use the sugar that circulates in the blood. Sugar is used by the tissues in the form of glucose, and, in order to produce energy, this is broken down into carbon dioxide and water. Any excess sugar in the blood is stored in the liver as glycogen.

If the islets of langerhans are not functioning properly, there will be a lack of insulin which will result in diabetes, a condition in which the blood sugar is too high. It is normally diagnosed through the presence of sugar in the urine.

When this chakra is unstable, a person can be subjected to rapid mood swings. There will be a tendency towards depression, introversion, lethargy, poor digestion, and abnormal eating habits. Its malfunction can lead to nervous instability and disease if the energies from the heart centre fail to be expressed on the physical plane. This centre interacts between the heart and the sacral centre, and if it is blocked, sexuality cannot be connected to love. When this centre is open, a deep and fulfilling emotional life is experienced.

Visualization with the solar plexus chakra

Sit down in your chosen place, either on a chair or on the floor. Make sure that your spine is straight and your body relaxed.

Bring your awareness into your solar plexus. Feel and visualize the organs that are housed in this part of your body. Imagine that at the centre of your solar plexus lies a golden yellow sun which is fed by the yellow shaft of light that you bring through the earth with each inhalation. As you feed your sun with yellow light, it grows and glows more brightly. You begin to feel all of the organs and glands connected with this energy centre starting to radiate the warm, gentle heat of life and vitality. With each exhalation, visualize the warm, bright rays from your sun reaching out to other parts of your body where there may be discomfort or disease. Allow the warmth and light to disperse any negative and unwanted energy in order that your physical body may experience vitality and health.

When you feel ready, increase your inhalation and exhalation, become aware of your physical body and gently open your eyes.

The heart chakra

This chakra is situated between the fourth and fifth thoracic verte-bra. It is associated with the mental sheath, the element air and the sense of touch. Its ruling planet is Venus and it is associated with the quality of harmony through conflict. The dominant colour radi-ating from it is green.

On a physical level, the heart chakra is associated with the heart and circulatory system, the lungs and respiratory system, the immune system, and the arms and hands. The endocrine gland attributed to it is the thymus.

The thymus gland is situated in the thorax, behind the sternum and in front of the heart. It consists mainly of lymphoid tissue and plays a part in the formation of lymphocytes. At birth this gland is quite large and continues to increase in size until puberty, at which point it starts to shrink. The thymus plays an important part in the body's immune system by producing thymus-derived lymphocy. It is claimed that through certain yogic practices this gland can be kept active, thereby keeping a person youthful and the immune system strong.

This is the centre through which we love. Love can be expressed on many levels. It can be purely selfish, demanding and constricting, or it can be compassionate and caring. The more open this centre is, the greater our capacity to extend undemanding spiritual love. When a person has transformed personal desires and passions into a love which encompasses his fellow human beings, animals and nature, the energies from the solar plexus are raised into this cen-tre. When this centre is open, we can perceive the beauty and spiri-tual love in our fellow human beings. Its awakening brings a great sensitivity to touch, and a detachment from material objects.

This centre is linked with the crown chakra and the dimensions of higher consciousness. This link can be strengthened through the practice of meditation.

Visualization on the heart chakra

Sit either on a chair or on the floor in your chosen place. Relax your body, keeping your spine straight. Be aware of the gentle inhalation and exhalation of your breath and the slow rhythmic beat of your heart.

From concentrating on your heart, move your awareness slightly to the right where your heart chakra is located. At first, this centre appears to be very dark, but as you inhale, a shaft of clear green light enters it horizontally and illuminates it. This enables you to perceive at its centre the bud of a pale-pink rose displaying two green leaves on either side of its green stem. As the green light floods this chakra, it enhances the illuminosity of the leaves. On your next exhalation, the green light expands and fills your chest cavity. In so doing, it brings into balance your negative and positive energies; relaxes your physical heart; rids your lungs and chest of toxins; works with your thymus gland by strengthening your immune system and creates a general state of harmony in this part of your body. If you are suffering from any form of disease in your chest, visualize this as grey clouds of unwanted energy which disperse as the green light comes into contact with it.

Relaxing in the sense of well-being that this colour brings, direct your consciousness to the pale-pink rose. Working with energising the heart chakra has allowed it to open its petals. It invites you to sit at its centre. As its pale-pink petals gently enfold you, you find yourself cradled in an aura of spiritual love – the love that asks no questions and is able to accept others as they are, without judgement. Listening to the voice of your intuition, you hear it telling you to take this ultimate and true love out into the world in order that it may be shared with those who are destitute, lonely, unhappy and in pain.

When you are ready, increase your inhalation and exhalation, visualize yourself standing outside the heart chakra and watch as the rose closes. When you feel ready, gently open your eyes.

The throat chakra

This chakra is the centre of purification. It is connected with the higher mental sheath, the planet mercury and has blue as its dominant colour.

On a physical level, this chakra governs the nervous system, the female reproductive organs, the vocal cords, and the ears. The endocrine glands associated with it are the thyroid and parathyroids.

The thyroid gland is situated in the lower part of the neck. It consists of two lobes, which are positioned on either side of the trachea, and are joined by an isthmus which passes in front of the trachea. The active hormones of this gland are thyroxine and triodothyronine. Iodine is an important element in these hormones. Their main function is to regulate the rate of metabolic processes in the body and they are necessary for normal growth and development, particularly in childhood. They keep the skin and hair in good condition and co-operate with other ductless glands to keep the endocrine balance in the body.

The parathyroids are situated behind each of the four poles of the thyroid gland. They are about the size of a pea and secrete the hormone parathormone, which controls the calcium metabolism of the body.

The throat centre is the creative centre, especially of the spoken word. In singers and people who practise public speaking this centre is larger than average, brighter and faster moving. This centre is sensitive to colour, sound and form and therefore very alive in anyone who is connected with creativity in any of its many manifestations.

Visualization on the throat chakra (1)

Sit down in your chosen place. Relax your body and quieten your mind.

Bring your concentration to your neck and throat. Try to picture the structure of your cervical spine and the muscles surrounding your neck. Be conscious of your larynx, tonsils, thyroid and parathyroid glands.

On your next inhalation, draw a shaft of blue light through the top of your head and into your throat chakra. As you exhale, breathe out the blue light from this centre into the organs, muscles, spine and endocrine glands situated in your throat. Allow this colour to relax and restore harmony to this part of your body. If you are suffering from disease in a particular part of your throat and/or neck, visualize the radiation of blue from your throat chakra concentrating on the affected part.

When you feel ready to end this visualization, gently increase your inhalation and exhalation before opening your eyes.

Visualization on the throat chakra (2)

Frequently, in esoteric teachings, the throat is symbolised as a bridge – the bridge that has to be crossed in order to transcend from the physical into the spiritual realm.

Sitting in your chosen place, make sure that your body is relaxed and your spine straight.

Concentrating upon your throat, imagine yourself standing at the beginning of a bridge; a bridge that is just wide enough for you to walk along. It is constructed of very pale wood with a handrail on either side. Looking up from where you are standing, you see the light from your throat chakra radiating the full spectrum of blue over the bridge. The densest colour falls where you stand and the palest floods the far end of the bridge.

As you walk along the bridge, through the myriad shades of blue, relaxation, peace and tranquillity pervade your being. You start to notice the effect that these varying shades have upon you. The deeper colours seem to work with your physical body while the more ethereal shades affect you emotionally and mentally.

Approaching the end of the bridge, you find two light beings waiting for you. They explain that their work is connected to alleviating the suffering of mankind by re-establishing harmony and peace. They place a chair beside you and invite you to sit and discuss any malfunction of your physical body. Having done this, they lay their hands on the parts of your physical body where you are experiencing pain and discomfort.

Closing your eyes, you feel a warmth spreading from their hands into your body. A warmth that starts to eradicate pain and disharmony. As you visualize your body, it appears to be transparent. You are able to see the unwanted energies that have caused you problems starting to disperse.

When the light beings have finished their work of healing, they remove their hands, but the warmth and sense of well-being remains with you. Standing up and thanking them, you now start your return journey across the bridge. On reaching your starting point you again become engulfed in deep blue.

Start to increase your inhalation and exhalation in order to reconnect with your physical body before opening your eyes.

The brow chakra

The brow chakra is situated at the centre of the brow and is the centre of visualization and perception, and reflects the twofold nature of the mind – the ego self and the spirit self, the reasoning mind and the intuitive mind. It is at this centre that the feminine and masculine aspects of a person merge into one, bringing about a spiritual awakening. The colour which radiates from it is indigo and it is associated with the causal sheath.

On a physical level it is related to the eyes, nose, ears and brain. The endocrine gland with which it is associated is the pituitary.

The pituitary gland is about one centimetre in diameter and is situated at the base of the brain. It consists of an anterior and posterior lobe, both having different modes of development and entirely different functions.

The anterior lobe of the pituitary gland is frequently referred to as the master gland of the endocrine system. The reason for this is that its hormonal secretions control the activities of the other endocrine glands. The many hormones which it secretes are under the influence of the hypothalamus.

The posterior lobe secretes two hormones: vasopressin which is an antidiuretic hormone, and oxytocin which stimulates the lactating breast to effect milk, and stimulate the plain muscle of the uterus during and immediately after labour.

Instability in this centre leads to tiredness, irritability, confusion and rigid thoughts. Imbalances can also lead to sinus problems, catarrh, hay fever, sleeplessness, mental stress, neuritis and migraine.

Visualization on the brow chakra

The brow chakra is often depicted as a two-petalled flower. This may be because this centre appears to clairvoyants as being divided into two segments, each segment related to one side of the physical body.

Sit down in your chosen place, making sure that your spine is straight. Relax your body and quieten your mind.

Bring your awareness to the point on your forehead between your eyebrows. It is here that the brow chakra is located.

Visualize this chakra as a long hall with a circular top. The circular part is filled with a deep indigo light and on the floor, embossed from mosaic, is a two-petalled flower with a golden centre. Standing in the golden centre is a music conductor, dressed in full evening attire, with a baton in his right hand. He invites you to join him. This enables you to look down the length of the hall. You discover that you are surveying your physical body but your endocrine glands have become members of the orchestra.

The testes are represented by the double bass and the ovaries by the cellos. The violins and violas stand for the adrenal glands. The solar plexus contains the brass section, namely the trombones, tubas, french horns and trumpets. The thymus houses the clarinets and bassoons, which are part of the woodwind section. The rest of this section, namely the flutes and oboes, depict the parathyroids and thyroid respectively. Surrounding the conductor at the brow chakra are the kettledrums and cymbals and behind him, acting for the pineal gland, are the rest of the percussion section, the triangle and tambourine.

The orchestra is ready – waiting for the conductor to give them the signal to start. He raises both of his arms, inducing peace and still-ness to the whole building. Lowering his baton, he invites the orchestra to play the symphony before them. Each section renders its scripted notes, which blend into an uplifting, healing harmony. The vibration created by the various instruments brings balance to the chakras and their associated endocrine glands which in turn enlivens and makes whole the physical body.

At the end of the symphony, the conductor lowers his baton and bows his head. You are left in the stillness and peace that follows.

───────── The crown chakra ─────────

The crown chakra is situated just above the crown of the head and radiates the colour violet. This chakra leads us into the eternal, infi-nite, supreme existence. It is the centre of pure consciousness. This centre is ruled by the planet Neptune and is associated with the causal body and with the pineal gland.

The pineal gland is a small reddish-grey structure about the size of a pea. It is situated between the under-surface of the cerebrum and the mid-brain, just in front of the cerebellum. Its main secretion is melatonin which affects the body's biological clock. The level of melatonin in the blood is highest at night, gradually decreasing during the daylight hours. This gland regulates the onset of puberty, induces sleep, and influences our moods.

When this centre is open, a person sees his/her spirituality in a very personal way – a spirituality that is not tied up with any dogma. This starts by them learning to love and respect every part of their being. If you have undergone surgery, love that part of your body that has been operated upon. This will greatly enhance the healing process. The same applies to any part of you that is suffering from disease. Love is a great healer.

Visualization on the crown chakra

Sit or lie down in your chosen place. Relax your body and quieten your mind.

In your imagination, place yourself outside the crown chakra. Slowly walk into this centre and lie down on the floor. You are free from all civilisation, alone and in silence.

The violet colour that radiates from this centre folds itself around you. It creates space and silent energy. It says, 'Love yourself, respect yourself, accept dignity and know that you are a microcosm of the universe'. Let go of time and space in this beautiful violet colour and feel at peace with all things.

Visualize yourself as a perfect spiritual being, knowing that you can be this being if you allow yourself to be. Realise that your thoughts can influence your physical body into health or ill health, whichever you choose. Welcome the emotions and feelings that you are experiencing at this moment. Look at joy and sorrow, love and hate, comfort and pain as if you are seeing the whole of your soul as part of the universe in which these feelings belong not only to you, but to all things. Look upon this experience as part of your growth pattern.

Be aware that your body is a temple in which is celebrated the transformation of earthly nourishment into the life-force energies. The spiritual energies have given unimaginable fine substances in order to allow the life-force to create seeds and plants, fruits and vegetables from which we gain this nourishment. In the violet colour of dignity, the transforming is like a holy communion on a higher level.

Your body, made of flesh, was formed out of the original seeds of your parents. You are now the conductor of this beautiful instrument. You are bathed in this violet light and are worthy to be chosen as priest/priestess of the universe. You are the physical representative of the divine world.

When you are ready, gently start to deepen your inhalation and exhalation. Reflect on your thoughts and experiences before opening your eyes.

—— Balancing the chakras ——

Go to your chosen place and put your body into relaxation using one of the techniques described in chapter 1.

When your body has reached a state of relaxation, bring your concentration into the base chakra. On the next inhalation, visualize a beam of pure red light coming through the soles of your feet into this centre. Feel its warmth and how it grounds you to this earth. As you exhale, let this colour radiate out into your aura.

Move your concentration up into the sacral chakra. Inhaling, visualize a beam of pure orange light coming through the soles of your feet, up through your legs and into this centre. Feel the joy and energy of this colour filling the whole of your being. Exhaling, let it flow out into your aura.

Bring your concentration into the solar plexus chakra. On the next inhalation, visualize a beam of pure yellow light coming through the soles of your feet, up into this centre. Feel this colour releasing any tension or blockages in this part of the body. Exhaling, watch the colour radiating out into your aura.

Next, bring your concentration into the heart chakra. Inhaling, visualize a beam of pure green light horizontally entering this centre. Feel it balancing the negative and positive energies in the body. Exhaling, watch as it flows out into your aura.

Shift your concentration to the throat chakra. Inhaling, bring a beam of clear blue light through the top of your head into this centre. Feel the peace and tranquillity that this colour brings. Allow it to release any tension that you may have found difficult to release. Exhaling, allow the colour to flow out into your aura.

Bring your concentration to the brow chakra. Inhaling, bring a beam of pure clear indigo light through the top of your head into this centre. Allow this colour to give you a clearer insight into any path that you may be following and the work which you have chosen to do in this lifetime. Exhaling, allow it to radiate out into your aura.

Finally, bring your concentration into the crown chakra. Inhaling, visualize a beam of pure violet light entering this centre. Feel this colour giving you the dignity that you should possess as a human being. Exhaling, allow it to radiate out into your aura. As it radiates out, it flows upwards and in so doing, changes into a pale magenta and then into pure white light. Remember that this is the centre that allows us, when we are ready, to be in touch with the spiritual aspect of our being.

Now bring your concentration into the aura that surrounds you. Feel it vibrating in harmony and filled with all the clear, pure colours of the spectrum. Feel these colours bringing health, vitality and well-being into your physical body.

When you are ready, bring your awareness back to your physical body; deepen your inhalation and exhalation and then gently open your eyes.

———————— Testing the chakras ————————

From the knowledge and understanding of these centres of energy, the colours which radiate from them, and their association with the physical body, we can begin to understand how important it is that they are kept in a state of harmony and balance. If they are not, then eventually the imbalance will manifest as disease in the physical body.

There are many way in which the chakras can be tested to discover whether or not they are in balance. One of these methods is through the art of dowsing with a pendulum, but this requires the expertise of a therapist because to dowse for ourselves is extremely difficult unless we can completely detach. I know, for example, that if I ask the pendulum if chocolate is good for me, it will indicate 'yes'. This is because my love of chocolate would influence the answer. One way in which you can test your own chakras is through a simple technique derived from kinesiology.

Firstly, join the thumb and first finger of your left hand to form a circle. Next, place the first finger of your right hand inside the circle formed with your left hand. When you have done this, bring your concentration to your base chakra and keeping your mind focused in this centre, try to break the circle by pulling the finger from your right hand through it. If you are able to break the circle then the chakra is weak. If you are unable to break the circle then the chakra is strong. Repeat this exercise with the remaining six chakras. What is important is that you remain focused on the chakra. It is very easy to shift your concentration into your hands. If you do this, the exercise will not work. It is the centres that are weak which need special attention.

– Visualizations for specific ailments –

Colds and influenza

This technique was given to me by my colleague who, when I contracted influenza, practised it in order to prevent himself from catching it.

Sitting comfortably, visualize yourself sitting in front of a roaring log fire and holding a large, flat sieve. The wires comprising the sieve are very close to each other making the apertures extremely small.

Visually take the sieve and place it under your feet. Then imagine yourself slowly raising the sieve from your feet, through your body to the top of your head. As the sieve passes through your body and out through the top of your head, visualize, as tiny black dots, any unwanted bacteria and/or viruses being trapped in the sieve. In order to destroy these, place the sieve into the flames of the fire.

Repeat this visualization as many times as you feel is necessary.

Fibroids and other growths (1)

Imagine that you are lying beneath a star-lit sky on a warm summer's night. In the stillness, your body relaxes and your mind is at peace. You watch as each star sheds a shaft of brilliant white light onto the earth.

From the stars, bring your concentration into your physical body. Allow your mind to focus on the fibroids or growths from which you suffer. Surround this part of your body in a golden orb of love and protection.

Return your awareness to the shafts of clear white light radiating from the stars. Visualize each shaft of light entering your body at every conceivable angle, meeting inside the golden orb that you have created. Visualize the power and intensity of this accumulation of white energy gradually burning away the unwanted mass of cells which have formed. The golden orb prevents this white energy from penetrating and destroying healthy tissue.

When you feel ready, end this exercise by stretching your arms up over your head on the next inhalation and lowering them back to your sides on an exhalation. Then gradually open your eyes.

Each time you practise this exercise, visualize the fibroids or growths shrinking until they finally disappear. These exercises can be practised in conjunction with any prescribed treatment.

Fibroids and other growths (2)

Sit down in your chosen place, making sure that your body is comfortable and relaxed. Quieten your mind and dispel all negative thoughts before bringing it to concentrate on your body.

Visualize the fibroids or growths as being composed of an army of very negative and cruel men who are trying to take over your physical body. Visualize them dressed in a dark, murky-red uniform. Now bring your awareness into your thymus gland, visualizing it as an army of positive, brave men, dressed in white, who fight for your well-being. In your imagination, take part in the ensuing battle. Watch the advance of the white soldiers upon the sinister red soldiers; look on as battle commences, picturing the defeat and abolishment of the bad army and the victory of the white. With the foe vanquished, picture your body restored to health.

Malignant growths

When you are sitting comfortably and are relaxed, bring your concentration into your physical body. Say to yourself: 'I love my physical body, my thoughts and my feelings. Through this love, all cancer cells are being eradicated from my body'.

Still concentrating on your body, picture your circulatory system containing minute, glistening, silver fish. Visualize the cancer cells as green algae. As the fish swim through your body, watch them devour the cancer cells. With the decimation of these cells, visualize your body being returned to optimum health.

When you feel ready, gently increase your inhalation and exhalation before opening your eyes. Repeat: 'I love my physical body, my thoughts and my feelings. Through this love, all cancer cells are being eradicated from my body'.

⸺ General healing visualizations ⸺

The temple

Sit or lie down in your chosen place. Make sure that your body is relaxed and warm. Look at the thoughts which enter your mind; let go of them in order that your mind becomes quiet and still.

From looking at your thoughts, bring your concentration to your heart chakra. This is situated slightly to the right of your physical heart. Visualize a shaft of golden light radiating from this centre into the far reaches of the universe. As you concentrate upon this shaft of golden light, you find it surrounding and gently lifting you out of the room where you are relaxing and into the vast space and peace of the universe. Looking back, you can see the planet Earth bathed in an orb of blue light. Travelling along the shaft of golden light, eventually brings you to a valley. Looking along the valley, you see in the distance a round, white temple. As you walk towards this temple you pass flowers and shrubs of every colour and description known to man; you pass animals, some grazing, others playing. On approaching the temple, you find seven steps leading to its entrance. Climbing the seven steps and passing through the door brings you to a round room. The floor is laid with multi-coloured mosaics, the walls are white and the ceiling is domed and constructed of interlocking crystals. In the centre of the room a fountain plays. You are not alone, but in the presence of the guardians of this place. They invite you to approach the fountain and to place your hands into the water. The feeling is of warmth and relaxation – a feeling so pleasurable that it entices you to walk your whole body into the water. The sensations produced in your body as it makes contact with the water release all tension, stress, toxins and discomfort, leaving it with the impression that it has shed an old worn out skin and donned a new, healthy, vibrant one. Stepping out of the fountain, you experience a lightness and a sense of peace and tranquillity.

When thanking the guardians of this place, they tell you that you may return whenever you wish. All that you have to do is to follow the golden shaft of light which radiates from your heart chakra. Thanking them once more, make your way to the entrance that leads to the flight of seven steps. Walk down the steps and along the valley until you find the shaft of golden light. When you have found this, allow it to bring you back gently through the universe and into the earth's atmosphere. When you have entered the earth's atmosphere it brings you to the room where you started your visualization. Here you make contact with your physical body.

Slowly start to increase your inhalation and exhalation and when you feel ready, open your eyes.

The wood

Go to your chosen place and either sit or lie down, whichever you find to be most comfortable. Relax your body, making sure that it is warm, and quieten your mind.

Picture yourself walking through a wood on a frosty winter morning. The ground beneath your feet is hard and the frost that covers the bare branches of the trees glistens under the reflection of the sun. All is quiet and still. Observing the innumerable trees that you pass on your journey, you stumble upon a very ancient one. You suspect it to be the king tree, the ruler of all the other trees that live in the forest. It is very tall and has an enormously thick trunk with large overhanging branches. When walking around and exploring this tree, you discover an opening in its trunk, just large enough for you to pass through in a crouching position. On entering the tree, you are at first encompassed by darkness which prevents you from surveying your surroundings. Gradually, as your eyes grow accustomed to the darkness, you are able to investigate the inner world of the tree. You discover an old, thick branch lying on the dry and leaf-covered floor. Upon this you sit while observing the various stages of decay that the leaves and objects surrounding you have reached. In doing this, you notice glints of light radiating from the ground. Searching for the source of these reflections, you learn that the ground beneath your feet is strewn with tiny quartz crystals. Taking one into your hands, you become aware that you are not alone but in the presence of the guardians who care for the mineral kingdom. In the silence of your thoughts, they instruct you to hold the crystal in the light that shines through the entrance to the tree. In so doing, you find that the light, as it enters the crystal, is split into the eight colours of the spectrum; red, orange, yellow, green, turquoise, blue, violet, magenta. This rainbow of colour dances on the walls and floor. You are further instructed to place your crystal on any part of your body where you are experiencing pain or where there is disease. Against the cold and dampness of the air, the crystal creates a warm, vibrating glow throughout your body. The soothing pulsation from the crystal starts to ease pain and to dispel the negative and unwanted energies which create disease.

When you feel ready, place the crystal back onto the floor. Standing up, walk to the opening in the tree and pass through it. On the other side, you find yourself back in the room where you started your visualization. Gently increasing your inhalation and exhalation, become aware of your physical body, and, when you are ready, open your eyes.

The following affirmation should be used at the end of each healing visualization, barring the one for cancer which has its own.

I love my physical body, my thoughts and my feelings. This love I perceive as a pale-pink mist which softly envelops each cell of my body, creating health, peace and harmony.

6

COLOUR

How many people stop to observe and wonder at the phenomenon of colour. It is something by which we are continually surrounded, but frequently fail to notice. We find it in nature; we use it in clothing and in the decoration of our homes. As we discovered in chapter 5, we vibrate to the frequency of colour, shown through its continual movement and change in our aura.

One of the most beautiful examples of colour is the rainbow. This arc of colour is caused by the refraction and internal reflection of light in raindrops. Another beautiful and awe-inspiring colour spectacle is the great display of polar lights, known as the aurora borealis. This is most frequently seen near the earth's north magnetic pole.

Colour can be perceived either as a pigment, which is a surface colour, or as illumination. To produce illuminatory colour naturally, the presence of darkness and light is required. Even though light and darkness oppose each other, they are still dependent on each other.

In 1665, Isaac Newton discovered that when light was passed through a prism it was refracted, producing the colours of the spectrum. The prism bent the colours by different amounts, thereby dispersing them and making them visible to the human eye. It was through his experiments that he concluded that white light was a mixture of many colours.

The colour spectrum can be divided into the eight main colours of red, orange, yellow, green, turquoise, blue, violet and magenta. Each of these has its complementary colour. Red is complementary to turquoise, orange to blue, yellow to violet, green to magenta, turquoise to red, blue to orange, violet to yellow and magenta to green.

Colour	Complementary Colour	Colour	Complementary Colour
Red	Turquoise	Turquoise	Red
Orange	Blue	Blue	Orange
Yellow	Violet	Violet	Yellow
Green	Magenta	Magenta	Green

The colours of the spectrum are found between infrared and ultraviolet on the electromagnetic spectrum and are known on this spectrum as visible light. Each of the colours has its own frequency and wavelength, the longest wavelength and lowest frequency being attributed to red. As we ascend the colour spectrum, the wavelengths get shorter and the frequencies higher; magenta having the shortest wavelength and highest frequency. Because of this, and coupled with the fact that we as human beings emanate colour, I believe that colour is a great medium in healing.

When we work with colour, our bodies become sensitive to it. This enables us to feel the vibrational frequency of each colour and, when using it therapeutically, discover which colour is most beneficial to us at any one time. When using colour in therapy, it is not only absorbed through our eyes but also through the pores of our skin; therefore, the colour of the clothes we wear has an effect upon us, not just psychologically, but also physically.

When using colour in visualization, it can be for the purpose of sensitising the body, for healing or for meditation. The visualizations given in this chapter are primarily for sensitivity and healing. In order to feel and appreciate colour, it is important to know each colour's attributes. These are given prior to the visualizations for each colour. To really get to know and love colour try to become aware of it, especially in the garden and countryside. Try feeling its vibrations through your hands and feet. Learn how it affects you. If you are attracted towards a particular colour, ask yourself if it is because you need that colour. If a colour repels you, again try to find the reason. It may be because it is associated with an unpleasant experience that you have buried in your unconscious mind. If, when you first start to work with colour, you find it difficult to visualize or 'feel', do not despair. Remember, practice makes perfect.

The colour red

Red is the colour which is dominant in the base chakra. It resides at the heat end of the spectrum and is symbolic of life, strength and vitality. In a child's aura, a great deal of red is present. This is because until the age of puberty, a child is still establishing its roots on earth and red is the colour which aids this process. As we mature in age, the presence of this colour in the aura diminishes and is replaced by the higher vibrational colours of violet and magenta.

Red is a very powerful energiser and stimulant, therefore not a good colour to work with prior to going to bed, especially if you suffer from insomnia. Because of its ability to contract energy, it is also not advisable for asthmatics to be constantly surrounded by it.

According to Ronald Hunt in his book *The Seven Keys to Colour Healing*, red splits the ferric salt crystals into iron and salt. The red corpuscles absorb the iron, and the salt is eliminated by the kidneys and the skin. This makes it a good colour to work with if suffering from anaemia or iron deficiency. Through its effect on haemoglobin, it increases energy, raises body temperature and improves circulation.

Red, when used with its complementary colour turquoise, can help in combating infection. Red increases the blood supply to the infected area; this aids in the destruction of bacteria. Turquoise helps in the reduction of any inflammation that may be present.
Psychologically red, particularly red light, can help to make us feel warm. Try sitting by an electrically simulated coal or log fire with the light on behind the coals or logs, but not the heat. You should experience a rise in body temperature.

Visualization with red (1)

For this visualization, you will need a square of red paper, cotton or silk.

Sitting quietly in your chosen place, put the square of paper or fabric at a comfortable distance from your eyes. Stare at the colour until your eyes become tired, then close them and try to visualize the colour red before your closed eyes. When you have achieved this, use your imagination to take this colour to any part of your body that feels cold. Visualize the part of your body that you are working with suffused in red light. Visualize the red light increasing the blood supply to this area, resulting in a gradual increase of warmth, to the point where the chosen area of your body feels quite hot. Stay with this visualization for as long as you feel comfortable.

Visualization with red (2)

In autumn, when the leaves start to change into their wonderful variety of autumnal colours, one frequently discovers not just leaves, but small bushes displaying all the shades of red that are discernible to the human eye.

For this visualization, find a red leaf and sit with it in a quiet, warm place. Begin by feeling the texture and temperature of the leaf and then try to feel its vibrational frequency. To do this, place the leaf on the palm of your left hand and place the palm of your right hand about three inches above the leaf. Concentrate on your hands for any sensations that are produced by the leaf. These could manifest in your hand as a change in temperature, a prickling sensation or even a dull ache. If you feel nothing, do not worry. This means that as yet, you are not sensitive to these vibrations.

Now try to tune in to the leaf's sound. Everything in the universe sings. The combination of these sounds produces what is known as the music of the spheres. Those who have been privileged to hear this say it is a beauty beyond description.

Open your eyes and look at your leaf, noting how it has been formed. Observe the geometric form of its outer edge; the thick and thin veins that run through it, and its overall colour. Survey the point where it was attached to the tree or bush and try to envisage how that tree or bush looked. Use your mind to explore the tree's yearly cycle of winter, spring, summer and autumn. Try to picture what happens to the tree during this time. Bringing your concentration back to the leaf, think about its function and purpose. Now that it has been shed, it will go into a state of decay. Is decay a final act or is it just a breaking down of an old pattern in order that a new one may be formed? Have you considered that the plant kingdom may have 'feelings' and a form of communication?

Through the many times that you work with visualization in this way, try to discover the answer to some of the questions posed and by so doing, gain your own inner knowledge about plants. Working with nature in this way teaches us to be very respectful of it.

Lastly, before ending this meditation, close your eyes and try to visualize the leaf before your inner eye. Try to be perfectly relaxed and objective when doing this because any form of tension will prevent you from achieving your goal.

The colour orange

Orange is the dominant colour of the sacral chakra. It is the symbol of feminine energy, the energy of creation. It is gentler than the dynamic energy of red but, energy wise, they are complementary. Orange is the colour of joy and of dance. It gives freedom to thoughts and feelings and disperses heaviness, allowing the body natural, joyful movements.

Orange is able to bring about changes in the biochemical structure, resulting in the dispersing of depression. This makes it a good colour to use with people who are manic-depressive or suicidal.

Visualization with orange (1)

For this visualization you will need an orange.

Wherever you have chosen to sit, with a relaxed mind and body, take your orange and hold it in the palms of your hands. Feel the skin of the orange, noting how thick and dented it is. Look at its colour to see if this is uniform throughout. Note the form that the orange has taken.

In your imagination, take the orange back to its source of origin; the tree upon which it grew and the tiny seed that produced the tree. For what purpose did the tree bear fruit? What would have become of the fruit had it not been picked?

Mentally, pass through the outer skin of the orange to its soft fleshy inside. Try to conjure up the taste of the orange, its aroma, and the texture and colour of its flesh.

Picture the orange increasing in size until it encompasses you, enabling you to sit at its centre. Looking around the inside of the orange you see the small clusters of seeds. Seeds which, if planted, will eventually produce new orange trees. Try to comprehend how such a small part of the orange is able to bear the blueprint for such a large tree. Is this, the seed, the very essence of the orange? If so, what is this essence, this blueprint, this energy. Each time you work with this visualization, ask that your understanding and awareness may be deepened.

Finally, try to capture a picture of the orange before your closed eyes. Visualize orange rays of light emanating from this fruit, into your aura. Hold this image for as long as you feel comfortable.

Visualization with orange (2)

For this visualization, try to find a deep orange dahlia or a picture of one. Place the picture or the dahlia, placed in a vase, in front of you.

Observe how perfectly and wondrously the flower has been formed. Look at the petals, observing the variance in shape and colour and marvel at the uniqueness of each one. Consider why and how the colour became manifest in the flower. Perceive how the petals are joined to the stem. Observe the fragrance being emitted by the flower.

Bringing your awareness to the centre of the flower, note the stamens, laden with pollen. Recall how this is collected and used by bees and how bees are instrumental in the cross-pollination of flowers.

From observing this flower, try to become part of it by visualizing yourself sitting at its centre, enfolded by its soft delicate petals. Try to feel the colour orange being absorbed through each cell in your body, filling you with joy and energy. If you suffer depression, allow this to be dissolved in the orange rays, thus enabling you to enjoy life.

When you feel ready, allow the flower to return to its normal size and become aware of your own physical body. Gently increase your inhalation and exhalation before opening your eyes.

The colour yellow

Yellow is the dominant colour of the solar plexus centre and is related to the mind and intellect. It represents the power of thought and stimulates mental activity. It is therefore a good colour to have in a work room or a study.

It is the colour of detachment and can help us to detach from obsessional thoughts, feelings and habits.

The yellow rays carry positive magnetic currents which are inspiring and stimulating. They strengthen the nerves and stimulate higher mentality. Yellow works with the skin by improving its texture, cleansing and healing scars and other disorders, such as eczema. It can also be used for rheumatic and arthritic conditions.

Visualization with yellow (1)

For this visualization, try to obtain a piece of sulphur. A good source would be a geological museum.

Sulphur is found mainly in the United States, India, Japan and Mexico and is often the result of volcanic activity. It is usually pale-yellow in colour but can be almost colourless. Apart from representing the quality of combustibility to the alchemist, it is reputed to contain healing properties. Many hot springs, respected as healing centres, have a high sulphur content.

Sulphur is traditionally used for colds, rheumatism, Hodgkin's disease, and relief of pain. In medicine, one of the sulphonamide drugs, known as M & B, was much used in the treatment of pneumonia and meningitis. Recent research suggests that sulphur can be used for arthritis, haemorrhoids and for skin and nail disorders.

In homoeopathy, sulphur is one of the most important remedies. It is used for numerous problems, including a wide range of skin disorders, burning sensations, and stomach problems.

Foods containing sulphur, which are therefore important for people who need this substance, are chives, garlic, horseradish, mustard, onions and radishes.

Sitting down in a quiet, warm place, relax your body and mind. Holding the piece of sulphur in your hand, look at it closely and try to discover how it has been formed. Look for specific shapes within it; observe whether or not the colour is uniform; find out if it is a hard or soft substance.

Gently closing your eyes, encase the piece of sulphur in both hands. Endeavour to decipher, through your sense of touch, its temperature and whether or not you are able to feel any vibration from it. Attempt to determine whether or not the piece of sulphur produces any sensations within your own body.

Through a technique known as psychometry, we can sometimes learn the origin of an object. In order to do this, continue to hold the piece of sulphur in your hands and ask it to reveal to you its place of origin. Sitting quietly, watch for any pictures that may form in front of your closed eyes or thoughts that may present themselves. If this is the first time working with this technique, do not be disappointed if nothing happens. Like most things, it takes time and patience.

Open your eyes and gaze again at your piece of sulphur. When you feel ready, close your eyes and try to visualize it, especially the colour. When you have obtained a clear picture, mentally take the colour of yellow to any of your joints which are painful or arthritic, or to any skin problem that you may be suffering. Visualize the healing properties of this colour bringing the afflicted part of your body back into harmony.

When you are ready, bring yourself back into everyday awareness and gently open your eyes.

Visualization with yellow (2)

For this visualization you will need a length of yellow silk or cotton.

Holding the length of material in your hands, observe how it has been woven and the feeling that it transmits to your hands. Look at the overall colour to discover if it is uniform throughout or has varying shades.

Place the material over the palm of your left hand and, placing the palm of your right hand about three centimetres above it, feel for any vibrations that this colour is emitting. Feel for any sensations of heat or cold. Now take the material and place it around your shoulders. With your eyes closed, be conscious of any effect, physically, mentally or emotionally, that this colour may produce. If you dislike yellow, ask yourself why. Sometimes it is joyous and uplifting to wear a colour one day and repulsive having it near us the next. When we feel drawn towards a colour, it usually means that there is a quality stimulated by this colour that we need.

Lastly, take the length of material and place it over your head. Open your eyes and look through it. Now close your eyes and try to visualize the colour. Imagine that you are sitting in front of an orb of golden yellow light that warms and vitalises your body.

Gently opening your eyes, be conscious of how this colours affects you.

The colour green

Green is the midway colour of the spectrum, being neither at the hot nor the cold end. It is the colour of balance, harmony and sympathy, and therefore has the power to bring the negative and positive energies of a human person into balance. Likewise, it has the strength to integrate the right and left hemispheres of the brain. The right hemisphere is the intuitive and the left hemisphere the intellectual. It can also balance the three aspects of a person's being, namely body, mind and spirit, thus creating wholeness.

Green has antiseptic properties which make it useful in combating infection. It can be used for detoxification and in some cases of heart disease and cancer.

Visualization with green (1)

Sit quietly in your chosen place, making sure that your body is relaxed and comfortable.

Closing your eyes, imagine that you are walking in the countryside on a warm spring afternoon. The trees that you pass are adorned with their new spring attire of pale-green leaves. The grass beneath your feet is springy and soft and gives the appearance of a carpet that has just been laid. The only audible sound is the gentle whispering of the breeze and the singing of the birds as they busily build their nests. Feeling the warmth of the sun upon your body provokes a feeling of peace and joy.

Following the winding path through the maze of trees, you become aware of the sound of water. At first it is barely audible, but as you progress along the path, it becomes louder and louder. On reaching the source of the sound, you find yourself standing in front of a cascading waterfall that has created a bubbling brook through some of the fields designated to cows and sheep. Exploring the waterfall you discover a shelf of rock extending behind it. The shelf appears perfectly dry so you decide to investigate further by walking along it. Passing behind the waterfall the noise becomes almost deafening but also sounds very beautiful. The reflection from the green trees and grasses as it passes through the water creates a hue of pale-green light at the back of the waterfall. Walking into this light you feel all toxins and imbalances in your body being gently washed away. This enables your energies to be brought into balance, which, in turn, creates a greater flow of energy throughout your body. The feeling of aloneness created by the water and the presence of the green light allows you space for reflection. A time to assess your own path in life; whether or not it is the correct path and where it will ultimately lead. During this time of quietness, insight and inspiration may be given to you. You may find answers to questions that have been puzzling you.

When you feel ready, walk out of the green light and out from under the waterfall. In so doing, become aware of your own physical body sitting in your chosen place. Before opening your eyes, sit quietly for a few moments, contemplating any impressions that this visualization has given you.

Visualization with green (2)

For this visualization you will need a sprig of parsley.

Herbs, apart from being fragrant plants, are now widely used in cooking and for medicinal purposes. Parsley is one of the most popular herbs and is a rich source of vitamins, proteins, iodine, iron, magnesium and other minerals. It can be chopped and eaten raw in salads, added to stews, soups, casseroles and vegetable dishes and used as a garnish. Parsley has the reputation of dispelling the odour of onions and garlic from the breath. Parsley leaves can be infused in water to make a tea. This is said to be good for the digestion, will act as a diuretic, and is favourable for the treatment of kidney and bladder complaints, arthritis and rheumatism.

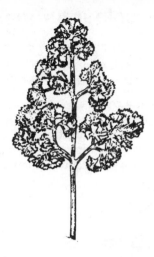

Sitting quietly, place the piece of parsley in front of you at a distance that enables you to see it clearly. Take note of its shape and observe how each sprig resembles a miniature tree.

Picking up the parsley, look closely at how the leaves are formed and how each one has a fluted edge. Try to discover how many shades of green appear on the leaves and stem. Are the outsides of the leaves darker or lighter than the insides? Do all the leaves bear the same pattern or are there slight variations? Is parsley an aromatic herb? If so, does it emit a weak or strong scent? Break off a piece of the parsley and slowly eat it. As you chew, visualize the green from this herb being absorbed into your body through your tongue. Visualize the energies of your body being brought into balance in order to create an inner harmony.

Opening your eyes, again contemplate the sprig of parsley. Now close your eyes and try to visualize it. Think about its medicinal uses and the substances the herb contains which promote healing. Think about its growth pattern and how the seeds which are sown in the darkness of the soil slowly germinate, pushing out of the darkness into the light of the sun. Can we liken ourselves to the plant kingdom? Our feet, being akin to the earth, planting us firmly upon this planet Earth. But, like the plant, from this firm foundation we grow and evolve towards the light of the spiritual sun.

——————— **The colour turquoise** ———————

The colour turquoise is derived by mixing together blue and green. Turquoise can veer towards either of these colours.

In healing, turquoise is a colour used to boost the immune system. Because of its strengthening effect upon the immune system, it can be used for infections, septic conditions and AIDS. As AIDS is a virus which destroys the immune system, endeavouring to strengthen this system with turquoise can potentially prolong an AIDS sufferer's life.

Visualization with turquoise (1)

For this visualization, you will need to make a turquoise circle. The size of it is your choice. To make the circle, take a sheet of white paper and draw a circle in the centre of the paper. You can use a saucer, plate or compass to do this. Using either crayons or paint, colour the circle turquoise. When you have done this, glue your circle on to a piece of cardboard and then cut it out.

Holding the turquoise circle comfortably in front of you, look at the colour. Try to ascertain what feelings this colour provokes in you. Ask yourself if it is a colour that you enjoy having around or if it is a colour that you feel indifferent to.

Closing your eyes, imagine before your closed eyes a sheet of paper, a pencil, a small pot of green paint, a small pot of blue paint and a small paintbrush. Using your imagination, take the pencil and draw a circle on the paper.

Next, pick up your paintbrush and using the blue and green paint, create a beautiful turquoise on the small white dish which is beside the paint. When you have done this, paint your circle with it, trying to visualize the colour with your inner eye.

When you have finished painting your circle, sit quietly and contemplate it in order to glean as much information as possible. If your mind wanders, gently bring it back to the task in hand.

When you feel ready to end this visualization, bring your awareness back to your physical body and gently open your eyes.

Visualization with turquoise (2)

This visualization is primarily for strengthening the immune system.

Our immune defences against infection depend mainly on the lymphatic system. This consists of lymphatic vessels which transport tissue fluid and lymph to groups of lymph nodes, which are widely distributed throughout the body, and then into the bloodstream. The lymph nodes, as well as other lymphatic tissue (for example, in the spleen, and tonsils), produce lymphocytes which have various functions; producing antibodies and attacking foreign and abnormal cells. The thymus is important in determining the character of lymphocytes, especially in early infancy and childhood, so that they do not attack the body's own tissue, but are ready to recognise and

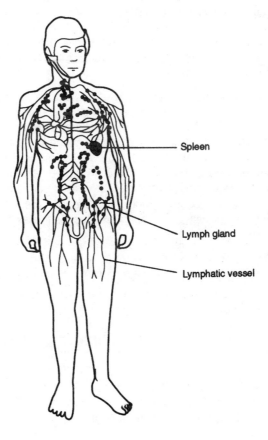

Spleen

Lymph gland

Lymphatic vessel

destroy invaders. When fighting infection, our lymph glands may become swollen.

Sitting quietly in your chosen place, study the figure in order to become familiar with the position of the lymph nodes and the lymph vessels in the human body.

When you have done this, try to recall the turquoise circle that you worked with in the previous visualization. If you find it helpful, use the circle again as a visual image.

Bringing your concentration back to your physical body, visualize the groups of lymph nodes as patrol stations and the lymphocytes, which are produced at these stations, as soldiers. Visualize the lymph vessels, which transport tissue fluid and lymph, as a running stream. The job of the soldiers at the patrol stations is to make sure that the running stream is kept clean and pure. Their job is to remove any debris from the stream. If our body is invaded by bacteria and viruses, the soldiers' work increases, making them tired and lethargic. In order to help strengthen them, you are going to bathe them with turquoise light.

Closing your eyes, visualize a translucent turquoise light before your inner eyes. When this light has become steady and clear, picture rays of turquoise light emanating from it. Envisage these rays of light penetrating the groups of lymph nodes, the patrol stations, in your body and strengthening the soldiers or lymphocytes which are produced and who work at these stations. As the soldiers become invigorated, visualize them working with great efficiency at clearing any debris which flows through the streams of water that they are in charge of. Visualize these streams becoming clean and pure.

When you are ready, gently open your eyes and believe that your immune system has been strengthened and revitalised.

The colour blue

Blue is the colour that symbolises inspiration, devotion, peace and tranquillity. For this reason, it is an excellent colour to use in places of healing, and during meditation.

Blue creates a sensation of space and because of this, a room painted in this colour will appear to be much larger. It is also thought to be a cold colour. The actual temperature, however, is not influenced by the colour itself.

Blue will reduce inflammation, and is used for laryngitis, sore throat and tonsillitis. It is also good for headaches and migraine. It is a useful colour with which to treat tension and insomnia.

Visualization with blue (1)

It is a clear, pleasantly warm day in spring and you are walking through a wood carpeted with bluebells. Finding a fallen tree trunk, you sit down and look at the spectacle of colour and splendour. Observing these flowers, you notice how wonderfully and intricately they are made. Each tiny bell possesses its own individuality of colour and shape.

Closing your eyes and visualizing one of these flowers, you find that the bell shape of the flower starts to expand, until it completely surrounds you and you find yourself sitting inside it. The stamens provide a pillow upon which you rest your head. Lie back and feel the softness of the petals encircling you like a soft mantle. The blue rays emanating from the petals play upon your body, releasing tension in your muscles and organs. Your inhalation and exhalation deepen as your body relaxes.

In this state of relaxation you start to think about the flower. The bluebell, like all other flowers, does not worry about the morrow, trusting that it will be provided for. How many of us have lost this trust and in so doing create for ourselves tension and stress through worrying what tomorrow will bring? Lying in the peace and tranquillity of this flower, are you able to surrender your worries and problems to that higher power which has created all things and trust that the things of tomorrow will take care of themselves? In doing this, we learn to flow with the energies of life which will bring us to the right place, at the right time, for the right purpose.

When you feel ready to return to everyday consciousness, start to increase your inhalation and exhalation and be aware of the flower of the bluebell shrinking to its normal size. Be conscious of your body lying in the place that you chose for this meditation, then open your eyes; roll over onto your right side and sit up.

Visualization with blue (2)

I have found that the most profound way of visualizing blue is to contemplate the sky on a clear sunny day.

Find a quiet, sheltered and sunny place out of doors. Lying down on grass or on the earth, look up into the vastness of the blue sky. Ponder the magnitude of space and wonder whether or not this has a beginning and an ending, or whether it is infinite. How little we know about the galaxies beyond our own and how microscopic we are in this huge cosmic field. We are as tiny droplets in a vast ocean but, as each droplet is an important part of the ocean, so we are unique and important in the great universal plan.

From looking into the sky, bring your concentration to the sun. Consider the important role that it plays in sustaining life. Without it there would be total, lifeless darkness.

Visualize emanating from the sun a shaft of golden light which stretches out into the immensity of space. In your imagination, see yourself travelling along this shaft of light, out into the universe. Feel the blue light in space surrounding you with a cloak of peace and protection. Listen to the sounds that each planet and star make, and the gentle modulating harmonies which create their symphony. Experience these sounds resonating with the sounds made by your own physical body. Each organ, muscle and bone echoes its own frequency; its own sound. Disharmony within the body happens when it goes out of tune. The cause of this can be stress, worry, diet or one's general lifestyle.

Try to visualize this vast expanse of blue permeating every cell of your body, releasing stress and tension and replacing these negative qualities with the positive ones of peace and tranquillity. Immersed in a state of tranquillity, try to hear with your inner ear the music of the spheres. Allow these multitudinous sounds to resonate with your physical body in order to retune and restore it to harmony.

From these wonderful sounds, bring your concentration back to the colour blue. Permit this colour to be absorbed into your body, mind and spirit in order to engender perfect peace.

When you feel ready, look for the shaft of golden light and allow it to carry you gently back to earth. Become aware of your physical body lying on the ground and feel for any changes that may have taken place within you.

The colour violet

The colour of violet pertains to spirituality, self-respect and dignity. It is related to insight and inspiration. Violet is frequently needed by those who have no respect for their thoughts, feelings or physical body – the type of person who is unable to love themselves.

The shining colour of violet can lift the prepared human being into a higher state of consciousness. Violet can lead us into a realm of spiritual awareness where it becomes the last gateway through which we must pass in order to become united with our true self or inner divine being.

In healing, this colour can re-strengthen a weak cell structure and restore energy. It can also help sciatica, diseases of the scalp and all diseases connected with the nervous system.

Visualization with violet (1)

We frequently talk about love; the love that we have for a partner, husband, wife, family and friends, but how many people truly love themselves. Before starting this visualization, go and look at yourself in a mirror. Tell the reflection that you see how much you love it. You may laugh at this suggestion and feel that it is a crazy thing to do but, in spite of how you feel, try it.

Sitting in your chosen place, visualize yourself wrapped in a length of violet material. If you have a piece of material in this colour use it to wrap round yourself.

Visualizing yourself enshrouded in violet, be aware of any feelings that this colour provokes. Ask yourself if it is a colour that you would enjoy wearing, or a colour which you dislike.

Violet is a colour that symbolises self-respect, dignity and love. What is your concept of love? Love can take many forms, be experienced on many levels and is constantly changing to the point where the state of ultimate love is reached. It is at this point that a person becomes love.

Thinking about love, are you able to love yourself. Also, what is your concept of self? When this question is posed, most people identify their self with the physical body. Perhaps this is the place where we have to start but, if we are divine beings that have no beginning and no ending and, knowing that our physical body perishes, what, then, is that Divine self?

Bringing your awareness back to your physical body cloaked in violet, with closed eyes endeavour to visualize this colour. Imagine violet interacting with your physical body; saturating every molecule and atom and suffusing you with respect and dignity. Allow this colour to extend into your emotions and intellect, thereby teaching you to respect your feelings and thoughts.

Before ending this visualization, sit for a while in silence, contemplating what you have experienced with this colour and what it has taught you.

Visualization with violet (2)

A crystal that reflects the colour of violet is amethyst. Amethyst is commonly found in Brazil, Canada, Uruguay and Sri Lanka. The name comes from the Greek word *amethustos,* meaning 'without drunkenness'. It is traditionally called the bishop's stone because in the Catholic church, it is worn on the left hand of bishops and kissed by the devout.

Amethyst is a powerful healing stone and comes in light and dark shades of violet. The lighter shades can be used for mysticism and spiritual inspiration, whereas the darker shades act as powerful transformers of energy. These darker shades work with the kundalini energy, balancing and stabilising the base chakra. The amethyst is a stone of inspiration and humility, reflecting the love of God. It is a wonderful stone to use in healing, especially in conjunction with colour healing. It helps both physical and emotional pain.

Sitting in your chosen place, gently start to relax your mind and your body.

Visualize yourself standing beside a giant amethyst crystal. Walking around the crystal you discover a door situated in one of its facets. This door has a round crystal handle on its left side. Take hold of the handle and turn it; push the door open and walk through the opening. You find that you have entered a crystal room, in the centre of which stands a chair.

After closing the door, walk over to the chair and sit down. Sitting and surveying this wonderful crystal room, you discover that it is bathed in a soft violet light which gently enfolds itself around you like a smooth violet cape. You start to feel the life-force that permeates the crystal and the soft, almost inaudible, sound which it vibrates to. As these sensations start to interact with your physical body you find yourself encapsulated in an orb of love and light. All the emotional pains and traumas that have been part of your life are gently dissolved and replaced with the vibrational force of spiritual love. This enables you to look, with love, at all aspects of yourself and creates the necessary space for you to be able to break and let go of all the emotional ties that are binding and stopping you from walking forward. Search in your heart for any emotional ties which you feel are no longer beneficial to you. With love, unveil these ties to the soft violet light of the amethyst. Watch them being gently dissolved in order that they can be reformed on a higher level of understanding. This action perfects within you a feeling of lightness, joy and well-being.

With these new-found feelings integrating into your everyday life, it is time to return to everyday consciousness. Rising from your chair, walk back to the crystal door. Turn the handle and pull the door open. Walk through, closing the door behind you, back to the place where you chose to practise this visualization. When you feel ready, open your eyes.

The colour magenta

The colour magenta is obtained by mixing red and violet. It is a colour which enables us to 'let go'.

On a physical/mental level, it allows us to let go of ideas and thought patterns that are no longer right for us. If we hold on to ideas and conditioning that originated in our childhood and/or adolescence, we become rigid and static, no longer able to grow and evolve. A lot of people find it extremely difficult to let go and flow with the tide of life, for this involves change, and change can cause feelings of uncertainty and insecurity.

On the emotional level, magenta signifies releasing irrelevant feelings. Perhaps we are still trying to hold on to a relationship which we have outgrown, or maybe we are trying to relive a situation from the past.

When magenta fades into pale pink, it becomes the colour of spiritual love. This is mainly used on the emotional aspect of a person. For example, someone who is suffering from a 'broken heart' could benefit from this colour.

In healing, magenta is used for tinnitus, benign cysts, detached retinas and, with its complementary colour of green, for some forms of cancer.

Visualization with magenta (1)

Going to your chosen place, relax your body and quieten your mind.

Visualize yourself sitting on a hilltop at sunset. The last rays of the sun create a spread of magenta across the sky. Looking to this wonderful spectacle of colour enables you to let go and just 'be'. Time and space dissolve creating a void in which you can find yourself. Let go of all your thoughts in order that they may become part of a firm foundation upon which you can stand. Standing and watching, you enter a state of nothing. From this state you are able to see a most exquisite and pure shining magenta. It looks like silver radiating out of space. It comes towards you and surrounds you. You are now able to see yourself as you are in this moment of time. It also allows you to see an image of yourself as a perfected human being. You ask, 'How do I obtain this state of perfection'? The answer given is, 'Let go; let go of all things that are no longer right for you and which prevent you from attaining this state which you desire; let go, in order that you may flow with the energies of life'. Inwardly, you know that the answer given is correct, but initially it creates fear and insecurity within you. Perhaps the first stage is to let go of the fear and insecurity. Allow these to become the stepping stones to the image of the perfected you that you have envisioned.

Pondering these thoughts, watch as the sun finally sinks beneath the horizon and the magenta sky turns into the indigo of night.
When you feel ready, return to everyday consciousness and gently open your eyes.

Visualization with magenta (2)

For this visualization, you will need a magenta-coloured rose. If you are unable to obtain one, then recall from your memory an image of this magenta-coloured flower.

For most people, the rose conjures up a picture of a country cottage garden. Roses are given as a gift for birthdays, anniversaries and to say thank you. Red roses are associated with love and affection, whilst the magenta rose is identified with spiritual love.

Sitting in your chosen place, if you have managed to obtain a magenta rose, hold it in your hands and concentrate on it. If you have been unable to find one, then close your eyes and imagine a coloured flower before your closed eyes.

Marvel at the way in which the tight bud has enfolded into what appears to be a spiral of petals. Notice how the sepals, which covered and protected the bud, have fallen away and lie drooping against the stem. Ascertain how each petal is formed and its overall varying shades of magenta. Observe how the light falls upon the rose, depicting shades of darkness and light. Look to the centre of the flower in order to discover its contents.

From the blossom, look at or visualize the stem and leaves of the rose. Note the thorns that grow on its stem, forming a layer of protection. If you are working with a live rose, you will find that its leaves are also prickly to the touch. In contemplating the leaves, do you find that they in any way resemble the petals?

If you are not already working with closed eyes, close them and try to visualize the rose. Does this flower remind you of the glorious warm days and balmy nights of summer? Does it recall any happy events of past summers?

Now visualize this rose in the centre of your heart chakra. Envisage shafts of pale magenta light flowing from the tips of its petals into your body. Permit these rays of light to extend beyond your body into your aura and then into the room where you are sitting. Visualize the room becoming filled with a pale-magenta light which changes the room's vibrations into one of pure love. Contemplate anyone who enters this room being touched by, and experiencing the wonderful atmosphere created by, this colour.

When you feel ready, gently increase your inhalation and exhalation in order to return to everyday consciousness, before opening your eyes.

Having worked with visualization on the eight colours of the spectrum, this chapter ends with a visualization which encompasses the complete spectrum and allows you, the reader, to choose, experience and work with the colour which you feel most attracted towards.

The night sky

Sitting in your chosen place, relax and gently close your eyes.

Imagine that you are lying in the middle of a field on a warm summer's night. Looking into the night sky, you perceive it as a large orbicular bowl of deep-indigo light, bespeckled with clusters of lustrous, glittering stars. As you reflect upon this scene, time and space stand still, allowing you to travel into and become part of this scenario. The deep colour of indigo protects and enshrouds you with a feeling of peace and contentment, as your journey takes you to the edge of what looks to be the brightest star. The brilliant white light radiating from this star appears to form a tunnel for you to proceed down. Walking down the tunnel to its end, the most wonderful sight is displayed before you. The white light has fragmented into the eight colours of the spectrum; red, orange, yellow, green, turquoise, blue, violet and magenta. Observing and digesting this panoply of light, choose and walk into the colour towards which you feel most attracted. Feel your chosen colour pervading your body and aura; feel its effect upon your thoughts and feelings.

When you feel ready, walk out of your chosen colour and back to the end of the tunnel. When you reach this point and look back at the spectrum of colour induced by the refraction of light, you observe that it is surrounded by an orb of gold. This golden orb beckons you to walk through it. Accepting the invitation enables you to experience the effect that the golden light has upon you. You feel its invigorating energy working with your physical, emotional and mental bodies. By the time you reach your starting point, the entrance to the tunnel of light, you are completely re-energised.

Walking back down the tunnel of light leads you into the indigo of the night sky. Cloaked in the peaceful tranquillity of this colour, you gently return to the hilltop where your journey began.

Before opening your eyes, take note of how this visualization has affected you physically, mentally, emotionally and spiritually.

7

MEDITATION

The explanation given in the dictionary for meditation is 'to consider deeply' or, 'an act of continuous contemplation, especially on a serious or religious theme'.

In raja yoga, the yoga of the mind, Patanjali, an Eastern sage, formulated eight steps by which an aspirant could reach the ultimate aim of yoga, namely samadhi or God-consciousness. The fourth of these eight steps is **pratyahara**, the withdrawing of the senses in order to still the mind; the fifth step is **dharana** or concentration. The stilled mind is now brought to concentrate on the desired object. This leads to the seventh step, which is **dhyana** (meditation), which culminates in the last step of samadhi or super-consciousness – a state beyond time and space.

The world in which we are living is full of strife, pain and disharmony. The pace of life seems to get faster with each passing year. I do not think that there is anyone who would not like to step aside from this turmoil, if only for half an hour, in order to experience peace, stillness and tranquillity.

— The physical and mental benefits — of meditation

Meditation is one of the ways in which this state of peace can be experienced. Meditation also improves physical and mental health and helps an individual deal with stress. It has been proven that:

- the heartbeat of meditators decreases on average by about three beats per minute
- the rate of breathing decreases
- the body's consumption of oxygen decreases by as much as 20 per cent
- blood lactate decreases – lactate is a substance produced by the metabolism of the skeletal muscles. High levels of lactate in the blood are associated with attacks of anxiety
- high blood pressure is returned to normal.

In order to achieve the benefits of meditation, discipline, in the form of regular practice, has to be established. For most people, the mind is their master, it is never still. In meditation, the aim is to reverse this process. We need to become the master of our mind. This is the only way in which we can transcend the mind and be able to experience the peace we are seeking.

Apart from experiencing peace, meditation is the way by which we can come into contact with our true self; that divine part of us that has no beginning and no ending. It also enables us to find our own inner centre where peace, love and security dwell.

—— Meditation and the chakras ——

When working with meditation, we activate the seven main chakras described in chapter 5. These can be linked to the rungs of a ladder; the base chakra representing the earth, the foundation from which we start. Through dedicated practice and discipline, we eventually arrive at the top rung, the crown chakra. It is here, in this elevated state, that we are able to see the meaning of life and the reasons why we chose our present path.

Through working with the chakras during meditation, they open like flowers. In Indian philosophy, these centres are depicted as flowers, each one having ascribed to it a set number of petals. Having opened them, it is very important that they be closed at the end of each meditation. These centres can be likened to doors, which if left open and unattended, present a wonderful invitation for any negative energies to enter.

To close the chakras at the end of each meditation, visualize a circle of light and a cross of light. Place a cross of light in the circle of light and use this as a golden key to lock securely all of these centres of higher perception. Working from the crown centre down to the base, visualize these centres as beautiful flowers, gently closing. Meditation can take many forms. It can be based on mantra (sound), yantra (geometric form), mandala (circular form), visualization, or silence, to name but a few. The technique that this chapter will be considering is visualization.

Visualization meditations

The prerequisites for meditation are the same as those for previous visualization exercises: your own special place which is quiet and warm; practising at the same time each day; whether sitting on the floor or on a chair, making sure that your spine is straight and consciously relaxing your body and your mind. Then be still and patient. Do not look for results because this will create tension within you. Trust that through your dedicated efforts you will reap your just reward.

Creating your inner centre

Sitting in your chosen place, start this meditation by relaxing your body and your mind. Try to let go of any thoughts that are not relevant in order that your mind can become centred on your body.

When all is quiet and still, imagine yourself standing at the end of a corridor. The walls of the corridor are white and smooth; the ceiling is the same as the walls, except for tiny lights embedded into its plaster, resembling distant shining stars. The floor upon which you stand is composed of small mosaic pieces giving an overall effect of swirling colour. At the end of the corridor stands a door.

Walking down the corridor towards the door, you become aware of the silence and peace surrounding you. Approaching the door, you discover that it is made of wood and has a wooden handle on its right side. Turning the handle and pushing the door open, you walk through into a room. The shape and size of the room is for you to envisage. Looking at your room, start to visualize it as you would wish it to be. Start with the ceiling; picture it painted with the colour of your choice; if you wish to have ceiling lights, place them there. Next, look at the walls. Place windows where you would like them to be and if you would like a glass patio door, visualize it. When you have done this, either paper or paint the walls in a way that would please you, setting wall lights or candles, if you would like to have these. If you have put windows in your room and wish to dress them, do so, either with curtains or blinds. Walk over to the windows or door and picture an outside scene that would uplift you. It could be the countryside, seaside, a beautiful garden, a forest or the heart of mountainous terrain.

Surveying the progress of your room, look at the floor. Decide what you would like to cover the floor with and in what colour, then visualize your decision. When you have done this, contemplate how you would like to furnish your room; perhaps you would like to have just floor cushions; maybe chairs; perhaps a table or even a bed to lounge upon.

When you have done this, sit down and review your creation. If you feel that something needs changing or you wish to add to your room, then do so. When you are completely satisfied, allow the silence and the peace of your room to flood the whole of your being.

What you have just created is your own inner space. A place that is known only to you and where, in your imagination, you can come at any time. A place where you can be totally alone or where you can invite by name a friend or master. A place where you can be truly yourself.

When you feel ready, stand up and walk to the door. As you turn the handle and open the door, look once more at what you have originated before walking through the opening, shutting and securely locking the door.

After locking the door, walk down the mosaic-floored corridor, back into the room where you started this meditation. Before opening your eyes, take a cross of light within the circle of light and place this symbol round each of your seven chakras in order to close them. Then, when you feel ready, open your eyes.

Encountering your true self

When your body is relaxed and your mind still, visualize yourself standing in a rocky alcove by the sea. You are alone except for the seagulls that cry and swoop overhead. Around you tower massive grey cliffs, indented by the pressure of the sea and clothed with ferns and wild grasses that grow from their crevices.

As you wander over the soft, silvery sand around the high grey cliffs, you discover an opening in one of the rocks. Walking though the opening brings you into a narrow passage. It appears very dark after the brilliance of the daylight. When your eyes become accustomed to the dark, you are able to see, from the small amount of light emitted through the opening, a winding passage. The walls, floor and ceiling are composed of rock and there are small puddles of water created by the sea at high tide. As you walk down the passage, you notice the damp, musk smell of the air.

Wending your way along the winding passageway, you note that it starts to widen. The light from the opening has faded but is replaced by candles set at intervals along the wall. On reaching the end of the passageway, you find that it has opened into a circular room.

Around the walls of the room are more candles whose flames dance in the circular pond residing at the room's centre. Around the pond are benches. You are alone; all is quiet and still.

Sitting down on one of the benches, you survey the reflected light from the candles swaying in synchronisation with the movement of air. In so doing, you notice that the centre of the pond appears to be radiating more light; a concentrated light which projects up towards the ceiling of the room.

As you watch, the light forms into a beautiful being which greets you before inviting you to ask any questions that you are seeking the answer to. In the silence that follows you are told that the answers to your questions may not be given immediately. They may be given through a book that you read, through a friend or in the silence of your own heart. What you are assured of, is that when the time is right, the answer will be given. On asking who the being is, you are told that it is your own higher self.

Before descending back into the water, this being radiates love and peace into your heart and tells you that you may return to this place at any time you wish.

Thanking this being, your higher self, and carrying the blessing of peace and love that you have been given, stand up and walk to the passageway that brought you here. Walking back along this passage brings you to the opening in the rock. Walking through this opening brings you back into the room where you started your meditation. Before opening your eyes, place a cross of light within the circle of light around each of your chakras in order to close them.

Listening to your inner voice

Go to your chosen place and sit down. Make sure that your body is comfortable and free from tension.

Focus your attention on your heart chakra. In doing this, you become aware that with each inhalation this centre expands until it surrounds you, allowing you to sit at its centre.

Observing your surroundings, you discover that the space in which you sit is bathed in a very pale-pink light. Flowers of all varieties and colours surround you and on the floor pieces of rose quartz crystal are scattered.

Sitting in silence, you become aware of a voice speaking to you. At first it is almost inaudible but, in focusing your attention upon it, you are able to decipher what is being said. It is softly calling your names. The first name you recognise, but the second is completely alien to you. On asking to whom the second name belongs, you are told that this is your spiritual name, the one that you have carried with you since the beginning of time. It is the name that the whole of your being resonates to.

Sitting and reflecting on what you have heard, you are shown in front of you large wrought iron gates. You are asked if you wish to pass through these gates. If you answer yes, they will open, allowing you to pass through into a very beautiful, large garden.

This garden is filled with a vast assortment of trees, shrubs and flowers, and at its centre a fountain plays. Other beings frequent this place, but the one that you recognise is the one by your side, the one who's voice has been speaking to you.

Together you walk to the edge of the fountain and sit down. Looking into the water you see your reflection and that of your companion. At first, the two reflections appear separately, but after a while, they start to merge into one image. At first it is difficult to comprehend that the vision you now see belongs to you. It does not look like the picture that you have of yourself. It seems brighter, younger and more relaxed. The eyes reflect great beauty and peace. Asking what this means, the voice beside you tells you that you have been allowed to see your divine self, that part of you which has life everlasting. This teaching is the answer to the question 'Who am I'?

Gently, the voice tells you that it is time for you to return to everyday consciousness. Leaving the side of the fountain, walk back through the garden to the wrought iron gates. Pass through these gates back to your heart centre. Slowly increasing your inhalation and exhalation become aware of your physical body sitting in your chosen place. Before opening your eyes, close down your chakras as described at the beginning of this chapter.

The crystal chalice

This meditation is ideal for the morning. It is a meditation for an increase in spiritual energy.

Sit down in your chosen place, relaxing your body and mind. When all is quiet and still, visualize yourself sitting in a glass chalice. This chalice is bulb-shaped, wide at the bottom and narrow at the top – similar to a brandy glass. The way in which it has been made enables it to reflect all the colours of the spectrum. As the light passes through the glass, the space between you and the chalice is filled with red, orange, yellow, green, turquoise, blue, violet and magenta, colours which are constantly playing and dancing with each other. The chalice is strong and forms a protective web around you and its colours of ethereal light represent your aura.

Looking up to the opening at the top of the chalice, visualize a shaft of white divine light flooding into your body through your crown chakra and radiating out into your aura. It fills you with energy and light, so that you are able to become a pure, clear channel for healing, a channel of light and joy. The energy which it gives also sustains you through your day.

This light continues to pour down until you are completely filled with light. It gives you energy, peace and joy.

When you are completely filled with light, spend a few moments in silence, thanking the spiritual world for this gift.

Gently increasing your inhalation and exhalation, close down your centres of higher perception described at the beginning of this chapter before opening your eyes and starting your day.

— Meditations on the four seasons —

Winter

Sitting in your chosen place, relax your body and mind and make sure that your spine is straight before closing your eyes.

It is winter, and the newly fallen snow lies crisp and white upon the ground, creating a blanket of stillness and silence. The bare branches of trees and stems of plants look stark against its brilliance and are bowed down beneath its weight. Small creatures have hibernated to dream of the advent of spring. Birds, which have chosen not to migrate, search for food in order to survive.

In contemplating this scene envisaged before your inner eye, search for what it is able to teach you. White is the colour of illumination, purity and innocence; of chastity, holiness, sacredness and redemption. When it is worn by a bride it signifies the change from single into married status. When used for funerals, it represents the death of the physical body, making way for rebirth into a new life.

Winter is a time when change is taking place within nature. All that which has decayed is undergoing transformation within the silence and darkness of the earth.

Do we as human beings likewise have our seasons? Can times of fruitlessness and desolation in our life be likened to winter and can these states be indicative to change; the breaking down into chaos in preparation for a new order to be established.

As you visualize this winter scene, try to ascertain what it is saying to you. Remember that this season of the year is a preparation for spring; for rebirth and transformation. All living things take time to sleep so that their energies may be recharged. Can this time of the year be likened to the fourth stage of life, namely old age. Is this a preparation for the transformation and rebirth that death accomplishes.

When you feel ready, bring your concentration back to your physical body, increase your inhalation and exhalation before using a cross of light and the circle of light to close your centres of higher perception.

Spring

When your body is relaxed and your mind at peace, visualize a spring day. The sun is shining, warming the earth after the sojourn of winter. The trees are laden with sweet-smelling blossom and the buds on plants are waiting to burst into flower. Birds sing as they put the finishing touches to their nests in preparation for laying their eggs. The heaviness of winter has been replaced with the joy, lightness and rebirth of spring.

In visualizing this scene, contemplate what spring means to you. When we have walked through a dark tunnel, emergence at the end of it can be likened to spring. We are able to look back and see the transformation that has taken place within us during the period of darkness, and the reason for these changes. It is like taking a deep breath of fresh air before continuing along the path of life. Joy and lightness are in our footsteps.

Spring is also the time of our youth. A time of discovery; a time of adventure; a time when we anticipate and dream about our future. A time of pain as we love and fall out of love. We, like the birds, long for the time when we will have our own home and bring new lives into the world.

Cast your mind back to your own youth. Follow the path that you trod from that time till now. Take from it all the positive things, learn from your mistakes and laugh at your mishaps. When you arrive at the present day, visualize how you would like to spend the rest of your life and see yourself accomplishing the tasks set before you.

When you are ready, gently increase your inhalation and exhalation and become aware of your physical body. Taking a cross of light and the circle of light, use this as a golden key to lock all of your centres of higher perception.

Summer

Sitting down in your chosen place, relax your body and mind and gently close your eyes.

Spring has passed into summer. The flowers are in full bloom; young birds are learning to fly; young animals are exploring the exciting world around them. The days are hot and endless, the nights balmy and short.

In visualizing this scene, what thoughts does summer conjure up in your mind. For most people, it is the time when they have reached their full potential. A time of creation, laughter and hard work; a time when the future seems aeons away. Summer can be related to the second stage of life; the stage when we are in full bloom.

Visualize the scene set before you and contemplate what it means to you. Visualize yourself walking in the country with the warmth of the sun playing on your body; the smell of newly cut grass and the beauty of nature in full blossom. Be aware of the affect that this has upon you mentally, emotionally and physically. Feel the lightness of your sparsely clad body and the energising effect that the sun has upon it.

When you are ready, gently start to increase your inhalation and exhalation, bringing your awareness back to your physical body. Close down your chakras as described at the beginning of this chapter, then open your eyes.

Autumn

Sit down in your chosen place and relax your body and mind.

Summer has passed into autumn. The leaves have taken on their autumnal colours of red, yellow and gold. The days are shortening and the nights lengthening. All of nature, her work accomplished, is busily preparing for winter; sleep and change.

In visualizing this scene, how do you look upon the autumn of your life. In ancient times, for a woman especially, this was a very important and special time. Having raised her family and passed through the menopause, she was able to assume the role of priestess. This was accomplished by transmuting the earthly energies into the higher spiritual, creative energies. Sadly, in our culture today, so many women feel that once they have passed the age of child bearing, their life has ended; they are no longer a valuable member of society. Unfortunately, the taking of HRT (hormone replacement therapy) prevents this transformation of energies from taking place. The taking of HRT may make a woman feel younger, but I feel that she is sacrificing the reward of reaching her full potential. In the same way that nature has her seasons, each one designed to follow a natural progression to the next, so have we as humans.

Sitting quietly, reflect upon this autumnal scene. How do you relate it to your own evolutionary growth? If you are a woman, can you accept the exciting prospects that this stage of your life can bring. Do you have the maturity to accept yourself as a priestess.

Are you able to look upon it as a time of preparation for the laying down of the physical body in order to pass into the spiritual realm. If we believe in everlasting life then this, like the passing of winter into spring, should be a natural progression.

Sitting in silence, visualize the four seasons and how one smoothly passes into the next. Relate this to your own life, contemplating what it means to you.

When you are ready, increase your inhalation and exhalation and close down your centres of higher perception as described at the beginning of this chapter.

— Meditations on the four elements —

We are told, and this I believe, that each one of us has a guardian angel; a being that takes care of and guides us during our sojourn on earth. I also believe that like us, all things living have a being that guards and watches over them. In this belief, I include the four elements of earth, fire, water and air. The collective name given to the guardians of these four elements are the **elementals**.

For some people, this could be a new concept, one that is difficult to comprehend. But, if we believe that God or the supreme intelligence which created all things allows part of the angelic kingdom to watch over us, is it not feasible to assume that He places the rest of His creation under the care of guardian beings.

Earth

To me, the Earth is a living, breathing structure. Unfortunately, due to man's thoughtlessness and greed, it is, through pollution and the destruction caused by robbing it of its oil and minerals, etc., gradually dying. If we wish this planet to survive, then we have to start treating it with respect and love.

Sitting in your chosen place, visualize the planet Earth. Start by surveying its outer crust, constructed of land masses, oceans and rivers. Below this is found a mantle of solid rock in which caverns and caves are formed and crystals grow. Underneath this rock is purported to be a layer of molten iron and nickel that eventually leads to the Earth's inner core.

This meditation will take you into the Earth's mantle of rock. To get there, you pass through the darkness of the soil where seeds germinate and where the chaos created from decaying vegetation is restructured into new life. Continuing through the crust of the Earth you find yourself in a cave, formed out of rock. The inside of the cave is dark and resembles a large sacred womb. At first you are only able to feel your surroundings because the darkness is too intense for you to see. Stand still and listen for any sounds; sense the atmosphere that surrounds you. Standing and reflecting upon your feelings, you become aware of tiny halos of light shining from the floor, walls and ceiling of the cave. The light that these emit into the cave enables you to investigate its source. You discover that the light comes from hundreds of crystals that are growing in the silence of the Earth. The collective light from these crystals fills the cave with a soft pale hue.

Lying down on the floor of the cave, feel yourself to be in the sacred womb of the Earth. Are you able to reflect back to the time before you were born, when you lay in the darkness and security of your mother's womb?

If you are a female, reflect upon your own sacredness in the ability to bring forth new life. Contemplate how the treatment of the body physically, mentally and emotionally during pregnancy affects the foetus that is growing within the uterus. Can these thoughts also be applied to the planet Earth. Does the way in which we treat the Earth affect what she brings forth from within her. Are we not upsetting the Earth's normal balance by the destruction of trees and the desecration of her oil, minerals and crystalline structure.

During a few moments of silence, reflect on these things and then bless the Earth and radiate love to her in order to help her cope with finding balance amidst destruction. Before standing and leaving the sacredness of this cave, thank the crystals and the Earth for any insight that they have given you.

Gently increasing your inhalation and exhalation, become aware of your physical body sitting in your chosen place. Before opening your eyes, seal your centres of higher perception as described at the beginning of this chapter.

Water

Water is essential to life. The rivers and streams can be likened to the circulatory system of the earth. The rain replenishes the earth with plants and crops and by filling the rivers and streams, sustains the life of the fish and creatures that live below its surface. Again, it is sad to witness the pollution that man has introduced into this vital element and the destruction that this has caused.

Sitting in your chosen place, visualize yourself in mountainous terrain, resting by the side of a natural pond. The stillness of the air enables the surface of the pond to resemble a shiny mirror which reflects the mountainous rocks and shrubs that surround it. As you look into the pond, you see also the reflection of yourself. The clear, quiet surface of the pond enables you to see clearly the rocks and plants which form its foundation. On a stormy day, the turbulence caused by wind and rain obliterates this from view.

Returning your concentration to your own reflection, look into your eyes. These are frequently referred to as 'the mirrors of the soul'. Can they be likened to the pond? When we are in turmoil and cannot find our way out of a situation, then we are unable to see our true foundation. It is obliterated by our thoughts and emotions. It is only when we are happy and at peace that we are able to see clearly. Then we are able to look into the depth of our true being, that part of us which is eternal. This eternal part is always present but, like the bottom of the pond, we are not always able to see it.

In a few moments of silence, try to find the depth of your true being. In order to find, we firstly have to calm the turbulence and then, when we are prepared on all three levels of our being, the door will be opened on to the next level of consciousness.

Fire

When reflecting on the element of fire, two things come to mind. Firstly the warmth and comfort that fire can give, especially on a cold winter night; and secondly, the fire of purification. When we work with meditation on a regular basis, our aim is to peel away the layers that hide from us our true self. During this process, we have to walk through the fire of purification in order that the dross may be discarded.

Sitting in your chosen place, visualize yourself walking to a small country cottage on a cold winter evening. The snow lies thick on the trees and ground, obliterating the winding country path and forming a dense blanket of silence over the earth. The wind blows cold, penetrating the clothes that serve to protect your physical body.

When you have reached the front door of the cottage, open it with the key provided and walk through into the hall, closing the door behind you. As you remove your outer clothing, you feel a sense of relief at being away from the cold night. Walking from the hall into the sitting room, you find a blazing log fire burning in the hearth. Sitting down in front of the fire, you allow its warmth to thaw your chilled hands and feet. The only light in the room is provided by the fire, which creates ghostly shadows upon the walls and ceilings.

As you sit looking into the fire, be aware of the colours produced by the flames and how the flames dance with each other. Visualize the warmth provided by the fire spreading from your hands and feet through your entire body. Be conscious of the sense of comfort and relaxation that it brings.

Lying down on the carpet in front of the fire close your eyes and contemplate the phrase 'walking through the fire of purification'. What do you understand by this? If a person is ill, sometimes drastic action has to be taken in order to 'burn out' the disease. Likewise, when we have chosen our spiritual path, we frequently have to pass through this metaphorical fire in order to purify the body so that the spirit can shine through it. At times, this can be very painful, especially when it involves discarding those things which are no longer beneficial to us.

When you feel ready, visualize the warmth of this fire purifying your own body for whatever tasks you have chosen to undertake in this lifetime.

Gradually start to become aware of your physical body sitting in your chosen place. Before opening your eyes, close all of your centres of higher perception, described at the beginning of this chapter. Now, with peace and light, continue your day.

Air

Unlike earth, water and fire, air is the element that we are unable to see. We can feel it but not see it. Again, it is crucial to life. As human beings, if we are denied air for longer than ten minutes, we die.

When working with meditation, we come to a point where we are able to accept our own divinity; the concept of a supreme intelligence and the integration of the two within each person. This does not mean that we are able to see our divine self but, like the wind, we are able to feel the effect that it starts to have on our lives. If one keeps a 'meditation diary', then it is possible to look back and see the changes that have taken place.

Sitting in your chosen place, relax your body and mind. Imagine your thoughts to be beautiful bubbles that gently float into the atmosphere and disperse. When your mind is quiet and still, visualize yourself walking across a moor on a blustery autumn day. Feel the wind playing through your hair and clothes and listen to its roar as it rushes over the land. Looking across the moor you see a church in the distance. As you walk towards the church, watch as the wind plays with the few remaining leaves left on the branches by detaching them and then sending them spinning to earth. The grass upon which they fall sways in time to the wind's rhythm, moving the fallen leaves as if they are figures in a game of chess.

As you approach the door of the church, you become aware of how, due to its age, it rattles and shakes as the wind plays round it. Finding the latch on the right-hand side of the door, lift it and open the door. Walking through the door, you find yourself inside a small country church. On closing the door behind you, the noise of the wind is no longer heard. All is quiet and still.

The church, although small, is very beautiful. The pews are made of oak and each one has a line of pale blue kneelers hooked on it. The stained glass windows throw coloured reflections onto the floor and walls and give variegated hues to the vases of flowers housed at each window. At the end of the aisle sits the altar, decked in green for the season of trinity, and upon the altar sits a cross and six white candles.

Quietly make your way to one of the pews and sit down. Reflect upon the scene that stands before you and upon the silence of this place compared to the roar of the wind outside. How can this be related to our own path in life. Has not each of us to walk through the noise and turmoil in order to find our own inner centre of silence; that still, small voice within. When we have been battered by the storms of life, how wonderful it is to find our own centre of rest and calm. To know that we can go there at any time and be completely alone, detached from the world. Like the wind, we cannot see it with our physical eyes, but when we have found it, we will feel its presence and the joy it brings.

When you are ready, stand up and walk back to the door of the church. Opening the door and walking through, you become aware of your physical body sitting in your chosen place. Gently start to increase your inhalation and exhalation before closing down your centres of higher perception described at the beginning of this chapter. Then open your eyes.

Evening meditation

To end this chapter, this last meditation is for use prior to retiring for the night.

Sitting in your chosen place, quieten your mind and relax your body.

It is evening, the last rays of the sun have sunk behind the hills, leaving the world wrapped in its dark cloak of night. The birds have returned to the trees; head beneath their wing, they dream of what the day has brought them. Domestic animals curl up in their baskets and in their kennels whilst farm animals bed down in their stalls. The night owl and other nocturnal creatures are the only souls about, on the prowl for food and sport.

The flowers have folded their petals, encasing within them the memory of the warmth and radiance of the sun. All is quiet and still.

In this stillness, reflect upon the day that has just passed, its triumphs, its mishaps, its sorrows and its joys. Take from it all that it has taught you and be thankful. Discard any negativity, anything that you no longer need, that should no longer be part of you.

Reflect upon your heart chakra. Enter this place which houses your higher or true self. Surrounded by the pale-magenta light which is filling this space, allow it to enable you to let go of anything that you no longer need to keep and fill the void that is left with pure spiritual love.

Allow this love to emanate out from your heart to fill the rest of your body. Extend it still further into the hearts of your family, friends and those you love. Ask that this love and peace may reach those places where there is war, strife, disharmony and tension.

Now place a beautiful blue cloak around your shoulders. Place its hood on your head and fasten it down the front. Visualize each of your centres of higher perception being closed and locked securely for the night. Wrapped in your mantle of peace and security, go to your bed and sleep so that your body may be re-energised in readiness for the dawn of another new day.

Good night.

8

MANDALAS

The word **mandala** originates from Sanskrit and means centre, circumference or magic circle. The two prerequisites for creating a mandala are a circle and a centre point.

The centre point symbolises unity, independent existence, perfection and that Divine part of us which is eternal. In some cultures it is the symbol of God.

The circle is the symbol of eternity; a line that has no beginning and no ending. If we observe nature and the divine order of the universe we will discover many circles. By observing space, we discover that the sun, moon and planets are formed in the shape of a circle. In nature we find the circle in flowers, which make beautiful mandalas, and in the formation of the rings inside the trunks of trees. In the Christian tradition, the wedding ring also represents eternity. In geometrical philosophy, the circle is the symbol of unmanifest unity.

The circle encloses a space. That which is inside the circle is protected and strengthened. This philosophy is used in alchemy and demonstrated in the old stone circles. The circle also poses movement. This is displayed in the sacred dances of the whirling dervishes.

Mandalas can be used in many ways, for many purposes. The intention of those given in this chapter are for the purpose of visualization. They have been drawn in black on white paper so that you, the reader, can colour them. This act in itself helps to cultivate the art of visualization, as well as being very therapeutic. The colour and complementary colour have been given for each of the first seven mandalas because these relate to the chakras described in chapter 5. They can also be used with the visualizations ascribed to each chakra. If you would prefer to use your own colours and not the ones suggested, then feel free to do so.

With each mandala comes an interpretation of its symbolism. When you first start working with the mandalas, it may be advisable to work with the given interpretation before trying to discover what each mandala is saying to you.

Perhaps, after working with this chapter for some time, you may be inspired to create your own mandalas. In whatever way you choose to use them, I hope that they give you as much inspiration and joy as they gave me when I created them.

The base centre

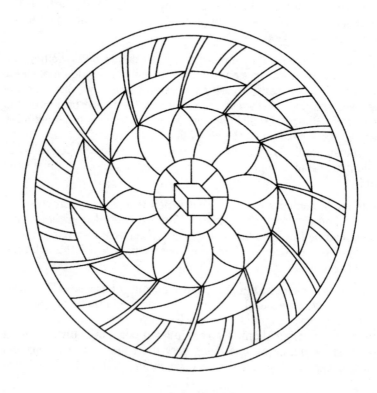

Suggested colours red and turquoise. Red should be the dominant colour.

Unless otherwise stated, always work from the outer edge of the circle to the centre. The outer circle represents where we stand at this precise moment in time. It stands for our present understanding and appreciation of life.

The cube at the centre of this mandala symbolises strength and solidarity. In order to climb the ladder of life, we have to start with a strong foundation. If not, the ladder will topple, taking us with it. In other words, we have to have both feet firmly planted upon the earth.

When you have finished colouring this mandala, position it where you can focus your gaze upon it without strain. Starting from the outer circle, try to discover the point that you have reached in your life. When you are ready to cross the boundary and move forward, look at the many paths open to you. Some will take you further than others. The names that you give to these paths are your choice. Try exploring them all.

As you near the centre, feel the web of your life becoming less confusing and more positive. Visualize your life starting to unfold like a flower unfolds to the rays of the sun.

Finally, reaching the centre of the mandala, visualize the cube as your strong foundation, which gives you the strength and support to walk forward. Having found your foundation, allow it to ray out and permeate your life.

Now close your eyes and visualize this mandala at your base chakra. Having reached and recognised your own inner strength, allow this to vitalise and bring into balance the endocrine gland and parts of the body associated with this centre.

Remember, the more you work with these mandalas, the greater will be their effect upon you. If, in your visualizations, your mind creates new interpretations, then write them down. Later, when you look back at what you have written, you will be able to see your progress.

The sacral centre

Suggested colours orange and blue. Orange should be dominant; two-thirds orange, one-third blue.

When you have coloured this mandala, place it at a comfortable distance from your eyes. Starting at the outer edge, visualize this as a wheel, the wheel of life. Having found our foundation, we must enter this wheel and allow it to move us forward in order that we may grow towards the realisation of our true self.

Moving forward towards the centre we find a circle of space. This space allows us to reflect upon ourselves; on our inner feelings. It permits us to muse on our discoveries and how these could bring change within our lives.

From this space, we enter the petals of the opened flower. To alchemists, flowers, especially orange and yellow ones, symbolised the work of the sun whose activating force brought about change. This was exemplified by the changing of base metals into gold. Whenever we start to work with ourselves, change is involved. This can at times be very painful. But having the courage to walk forward through the pain reaps a wonderful harvest. By walking forward and flowing with the energies of life, we are able to transform our own base metal into gold.

Looking to the outer petals of the flower, we find eight shafts of light radiating out into the mandala. Eight stands for stability, harmony and rebirth. In the middle ages, eight was a symbol of the waters of baptism. Water is the element associated with this chakra and we can use this for our own baptism into rebirth.

Eight also represents the balance of opposites. The energy of the sacral chakra is feminine. Are we able to balance this with the masculine energy of the base chakra in order to create wholeness?

Having reached the centre, take this mandala into your sacral chakra, visualizing it creating joy and harmony to all the parts of your body that it is associated with.

The solar plexus centre

Suggested colours yellow and violet. It is suggested that two-thirds yellow to one-third violet be used.

When you have coloured this mandala, place it at a comfortable viewing distance from your eyes. Standing at the outer edge of the mandala, perceive the circle being divided into four quadrants, each quadrant containing four objects. The four quadrants can stand for boundaries in our life, the four seasons of the year or the four directions of orientation. Contemplate which of these is relevant to you. In each quadrant we find two eight-spoked wheels. These symbolise the sun as the divine instigator of endless change. The element associated with this centre is fire. When we undergo change, we often have to go through the fire of purification.

Directing our gaze towards the centre, we encounter the circle of space, again divided into four quadrants. Four is the number of balance and wholeness. Do you feel that your life is in balance and whole or are you again creating boundaries out of the fear to change?

Passing through the space you are able to perceive the sun at the centre of the mandala. From the sun eight smaller beams of light ray out to fill the inner circle. These eight rays reveal the strong influence that the true self, represented by the sun, has upon us. If we listen, we are able to hear our true self guiding and helping us through our intuition. How easy it is to distrust this. In order to grow we have to learn to listen and to trust. Intellectual knowledge does not always lead us in the right direction. Our intuition does.

When our attention is finally focused upon the central sun, its warmth and light can banish dark corners of fear and hate and remove boundaries in order that we can become integrated into the whole.

Sitting quietly, visualize this mandala in your solar plexus. Allow the warm radiant rays from the sun to spread into every part of your body transforming sickness into health and fear into love.

The heart centre

Suggested colours green and magenta. The mandala should contain two-thirds green and one-third magenta.

When you have coloured the mandala, place it where you can study it without strain.

Starting at the outer edge of the mandala, one finds a circle of hearts. Hearts in most cultures are the symbol of love. Love can be experienced on many levels. When it is symbolised on the outer ring of a mandala it is indicative of intellectual, physical or emotional love. It is so easy to say that we love someone, and not mean it or have a true understanding of what we are saying.

Moving from the outer edge to the centre of the circle we again find the open flower. In some religious traditions, flowers represent the womb that nurtures the divine child. Flowers are also given as an expression of love. When we give flowers to a person whom we love, the love that we are expressing has passed beyond the intellectual onto a level of deeper understanding.

When we reach the centre, again the flower is captured but in a smaller form and with twelve petals. Twelve is symbolic of cosmic order. It is also related to the passage of time that must be endured before something new comes into being. Here, the new thing that manifests is the understanding and acceptance of spiritual love.

Spiritual love is the highest form of love known and springs from our own inner centre. Once we have made contact with this, we become love and therefore no longer have to think about it. It radiates from the very essence of our being, surrounding all those with whom we come into contact.

Close your eyes and visualize this mandala at your own heart centre. Allow the petals of love to spread throughout your own body and then into those dark places in the world where there is war, famine and disasters.

The throat centre

Suggested colours blue and orange. The mandala should contain two-thirds blue and one-third orange.

After colouring your mandala, place it where you can look at it without straining your eyes.

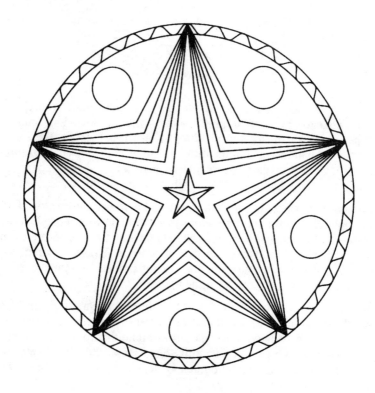

Starting from the outer circle of the mandala, we observe a five-pointed star. This resembles a human being standing firmly on the ground with feet apart and arms outstretched. It is representative of a person who is well grounded.

Around the five-pointed star appear five circles. These are for protection, and are indicative of wholeness. When we work to gain spiritual knowledge and insight and we use this for the good of our fellow beings, then we are protected by the hierarchy and gently guided towards becoming a whole person, one who has integrated body, mind and spirit.

Looking to the centre of the mandala, we find a smaller five-pointed star. Paracelsus, who was an alchemist and worked with colour healing, believed that our true eternal self resembled a star within us: the star that leads man towards great wisdom and ultimate reality. As we gaze at this central star, let us ask that we may be guided towards self-realisation.

Closing your eyes, visualize this mandala at your throat centre. Contemplate its meaning and ask yourself if you are ready to cross the bridge that leads from the physical realm and beyond.

The brow centre

Suggested colours indigo and gold. The mandala should contain two-thirds indigo and one-third gold.

When you have finished colouring this mandala, place it where you are able to look at it without strain.

Starting from the outer rim, the outer circle is composed of triangles. The triangle has three equal sides which, when joined, become one. Here it represents the union of the body, mind and spirit to wholeness. The triangle can also be an indicator of direction. In this mandala, the triangles are pointing outwards into the universe. At this time in the earth's evolution, it is important that we pour love and friendship from our own inner centre into the world.

As our gaze circles the mandala, we find two petals radiating out from the centre. This is the symbol for the brow chakra and represents the opposing forces found in each of us; the masculine and feminine, negative and positive, yin and yang. It is at this chakra that these become united through spiritual love, illustrated by the petals of the flower in the inner circle.

Shifting our gaze to the centre, we find the Taoistic T'ai Chi mandala, which shows the union of the opposing energies found within us. From the centre radiates two shafts of light each carrying a smaller version of the central mandala. Again, two depicts the division of the whole into a state of polarity. The two smaller Taoist mandalas again speak of uniting the opposing energies within us.

We have already ascertained that the circle is symbolic of the whole, that it is eternal with no beginning and no ending. This mandala speaks about dividing the circle into the two polarities of conscious and unconscious mind and then transcending both of these in order to unite them into the circle of the whole. By doing this, we obtain cosmic or God-consciousness.

When you feel ready, close your eyes and visualize this mandala at your brow centre. Try to look at the divisions in your life and ask yourself if there is a way that these can be unified. Now try to discover what this mandala means to you personally.

The crown centre

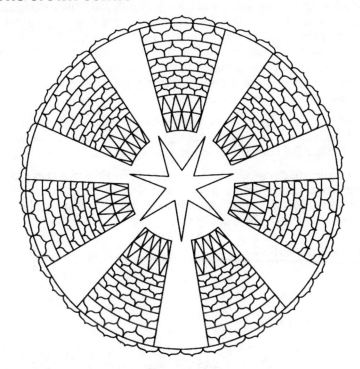

Suggested colours violet and yellow. The mandala should contain two-thirds violet and one-third yellow.

When you have finished colouring this mandala, place it where you are able to look at it comfortably.

The crown chakra is the centre of God-consciousness. Looking at the mandala we see many petals. These portray the thousand-petalled lotus, the symbol for this centre. A thousand stands for infinity. Once we have become one with the ultimate reality, time stands still; all divisions cease; we just become.

Looking towards the centre of the mandala, we find two sets of triangles – one set pointing towards the centre and the second set pointing towards the outer periphery. As we have already discovered, the triangle can be directional. The triangles pointing towards the centre are directing us towards the inner light whilst the outer ones are guiding that light into infinity.

At the centre is the seven-pointed star. Seven is associated with orientation and the designation of time. It also denotes the completion of a cycle of time. In Genesis we read that God created the heavens and the earth in six days and on the seventh he rested. The seventh day of rest symbolises completion. In the tradition of the goddess, the number three was ascribed to the female and four to the male. Therefore seven stood for the integration of these two energies, again creating a sacred wholeness.

From the central star rays out seven shafts of light into infinity. Once we have attained this state of being, namely God-consciousness, we become that light that shines out into the world for all to see.

When you are ready, close your eyes and visualize this mandala at your crown centre. Be open to what it has to teach you, knowing that when you are ready mentally, physically and spiritually, its inner secrets will be revealed to you.

Balance within

Choose your own colours for this and the following four mandalas.

With the seven preceding mandalas, we have worked from the outer periphery towards the centre. The next two mandalas encourage you to work from the centre outwards.

Once we have discovered our own inner centre, we find absolute security and undeniable love and peace. We can only find this by exercising discipline in our lives, allowing room for change and being prepared to flow with the tide of life. None of these things is easy. If they were, we would not appreciate the treasure that awaits us at the end of our labours.

When you have completed colouring this mandala, place it where it can be easily seen.

At the centre of this mandala we find a cross. It is made from a vertical and horizontal line and is reminiscent of the form of the human body, standing in perfect balance. The vertical line can be likened to a ladder, that which we have climbed in order to reach our inner centre. The horizontal line resembles the bridge that we crossed to bring us from the physical into the spiritual realm. From the cross, four shafts of light shine through us into the universe. Each of these shafts stands for a discipline that we have enacted in order to reach our goal. These could be eating less, talking less, sleeping less and meditating more.

Looking outwards from our centre we find the open petals of a flower, symbolic of the flowering of our own spiritual love. This flower is encased in a square, the sign of the firmness, stability and balance that we have gained through our efforts. This is exemplified by the square's relationship to the number four which again suggests wholeness, balance and completion.

Looking beyond the square, we find the eight-spoked wheel. Because this is the symbol of the sun, the divine instigator of change, it speaks to us of the changes that we have had to make to allow us to stand at our present position in life. We also find the triangle amidst the eight-spoked wheels, directing spiritual love from the centre out into the world.

Looking to the outer circle of the mandala we again find a cross. This time it represents the many crossroads that we encountered and the suffering endured as we peeled off the many layers that shielded our true self.

Closing your eyes, visualize this mandala in front of you. Contemplate the explanation that has been given and whether or not this has any meaning for you. Quietening your mind and listening to your own inner self, find out what this mandala says to you.

Our divine self

When you have finished colouring this mandala, place it where you can observe it without strain to your body.

Starting at the centre, we find an angel. Each of us has an angel within. This angel represents the eternal part of us that has no beginning and no ending. This being is seen enclosed in a six-pointed star, the light of which rays out to the universe. This central star sits at the centre of a second six-pointed star. Stars produce light; light which, metaphorically speaking, helps to guide us to our true self, the angel that is in each one of us. The number six is derived from two and three. In Greek philosophy, two is attributed

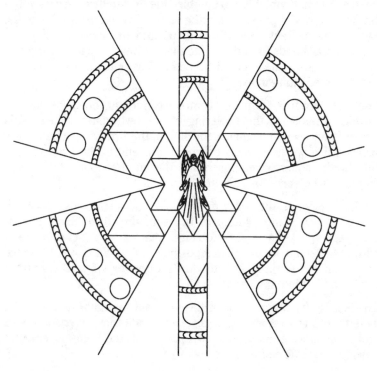

to the female energy and three to the masculine. By multiplying these numbers to produce six, we join the masculine and feminine energy to create wholeness. Our own angel or true self is neither male nor female but a perfect integrated combination of the two energies. Six also stands for perfection. When we have reached the state of wholeness, we have also reached perfection.

Directing our gaze to the outer circle we find four groups of three circles and two single circles. The number one stands for individuality and for the initiation of a process. In order to find our inner self, we have initially to start to look at ourselves in order to find the path to the wholeness that we are seeking. This can be a very lonely time because the person seeking often has to stand alone. When we eventually reach our goal, and this can take many lifetimes, we become complete. This is shown by the four groups of three circles. Three is a number of completion. Here it is indicative of our body, mind and spirit becoming one.

Sitting quietly, visualize this mandala before your inner eye. Explore its meaning for you. As you walk along your own path in life, and if you continue to work with mandala, new ideas and thoughts will present themselves to you. This is part of your growth and development towards the centre of the mandala.

Life

After colouring this mandala, place it where you can contemplate it in comfort and without strain.

Around the edge of this mandala are numerous petals. Petals are just one small part of the whole plant. Have you considered that each human being could also be part of a greater whole? Patanjali, a great Eastern sage, likened human beings to tiny drops of water that eventually become integrated into the sea. If we liken ourselves to the drops of water, what can we liken to the sea?

Passing over the petals to the outer circle, we find ten flowers. Ten is a number relating to morality and is the traditional number of perfection. The blooming of flowers heralds spring, the time of rebirth and renewal. Several years ago, I heard a talk given by Sir George Trevelyan in which he referred to the petals of a flower as metamorphosed leaves. In order to reach perfection, we have to undergo metamorphosis. Most of us are still in the chrysalis stage,

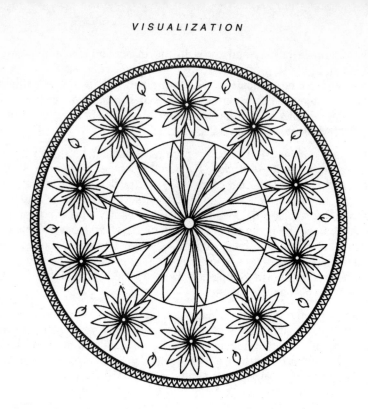

awaiting the advent of spring in order that we may emerge as a divine being.

As you contemplate these flowers, observe how their stems reach to the central part of the mandala. The central part of a twelve-petalled flower. Can this central flower be that divine nectar which nourishes all living things? Can it be the sea from which each tiny droplet is born, in order that it may return once more to its source of origin?

Sitting quietly, contemplate on these thoughts and try to find out what this mandala is saying to you.

Movement

When you have finished colouring this mandala place it where you can view it comfortably.

This mandala is based on the number 6, the number of creativity and equilibrium. When contemplating the universe, we find ordered movement, each planet and star obeying the law of the cosmos as it moves through space. When we look at this mandala, maybe we can liken it to the universe and find within it cosmic order. Can we then look at our own lives to bring order where there is chaos? When we start to work with ourselves, the things that are no longer relevant in our lives start to break down into chaos. This can be a very uncomfortable and insecure time, but out of the chaos a new order materialises, often on the next higher level of development. If we are working towards finding our own central divine point, then we, like the circles in the mandala, will be protected.

This mandala also speaks of joy. The joy that the whirling dervishes experience as they dance their sacred dance. With that joy comes peace and protection. Following with our eyes the dance of the inner circles leads us to three central circles around which the others are turning. These again represent that unity of body, mind and spirit which comes when we find our own inner peace and joy.

When working with this mandala, take note of what you experience and what it is saying to you.

Let the light shine

When you have finished colouring this mandala, place it where you can gaze at it without strain.

When first looking at this mandala, it appears to be made from two circles from which project the sun, moon and stars. Look more closely and you will find that these circles dissolve, allowing the central light to radiate out into the far corners of the earth. When at last we have found our own true inner light, everything that is no longer applicable to us dissolves in its brilliance and love.

This mandala speaks of light, that divine light, which shines out into the darkness. In some religions it is referred to as 'the light of the world'. At the top of the mandala is an eight-pointed rising star. This signifies rebirth from the old into something new.

Every 2000 years, the Earth and its occupants develop into the next evolutionary pattern. This is the meaning of the 'new age' of which we hear so much talked about. For those of us who have chosen to go forward, many changes will be demanded in order that we may become one with that light.

Closing your eyes, visualize this flame centred in your heart. Allow it to grow until you are sitting at its centre. Now send the shafts of light that radiate from it to anyone whom you know to be ill, in trouble, lonely or depressed; send it to places in the world where there is famine, war and unrest; send it to those who are seeking, in order that they may find; finally grant to yourself the love, peace and contentment which stems from your inner light.

When you are ready, gently increase your inhalation and exhalation and open your eyes. Looking once more to the mandala, let your own light shine out to all those that you come into contact with this day.

When you have finished colouring and working with the twelve mandalas given in this book, try creating your own. They need not be geometrically accurate or complex. Start by drawing a circle. If you do not possess a compass, use a saucer or a plate to draw round. Filling the circle can take many forms. You can use geometric forms, shapes, animals or plants. Another way is to fill your circle with colour. Choose the colours which you feel attracted towards. Then sit down in a place that is free from noise and let your hands do the colouring. You do not have to create a beautiful picture, it can be completely abstract. It may represent your present feelings or it may portray a much deeper aspect of your being.

Keep any mandalas that you create because looking back over them can produce great insight; they can also reveal your progress. For whatever the reason you choose to work with mandalas, it is most important that you enjoy doing them and gain a sense of fun and laughter. Remember the old saying, 'Laughter is the best medicine'.

FURTHER READING

Chopra, Deepak, *Quantum Healing*, Bantam, 1989.

Dethlefsen, Thorwald, *The Healing Power of Illness*, Element, 1990.

Downer, Jane, *Shiatsu: Headway Lifeguides*, Headway, 1992.

Gerber, Richard, *Vibrational Medicine*, Bear & Co, 1954.

Harvey, Eliana and Oates, Mary Jane, *Acupressure: Headway Lifeguides*, Headway, 1994.

MacEoin, Beth, *Homoeopathy: Headway Lifeguides*, Headway, 1992.

Mira, Silva and Mehta, Shyam, *Yoga The Iyengar Way*, Dorling Kindersley, 1990.

Ramacharaka, Yogi, *The Science of Breath*, L. N. Fowler & Co Ltd, 1960.

Stormer, Chris, *Reflexology: Headway Lifeguides*, Headway, 1992.

Wills, P., *Colour Therapy*, Element, 1993.

Wills, P., *The Reflexology Manual*, Hodder Headline, 1995.

Wills, P. and Gimbel, T., *16 Steps to Health and Energy*, Quantam, 1992.

INDEX

MASSAGE

DENISE BROWN

Massage has always been a popular technique used for the relief of stress, for sports injuries and to develop relationships.

This new book gives a complete guide to massage for the general reader. It is also suitable as an introductory guide for students training in massage, sports therapies or beauty therapy.

Denise Brown provides a practical, simple and effective guide explaining the benefits of massage and showing the main methods used for different parts of the body. The book is illustrated with many fully labelled and informative diagrams.

MEDITATION

JAMES HEWITT

Meditation helps you to maintain physical health and mental clarity with equanimity. It is the key technique in the search for higher consciousness and, as such, plays a vital role in many of the world's religions and the pursuit of psycho-physical relaxation.

James Hewitt provides a clear, concise and practical guide to meditation as practised in both East and West. He is not solely concerned with one tradition or school, but explores the different methods of meditation and encourages you to experiment to find the one that suits you best.

RELAXATION

JAMES HEWITT

This book explains the benefits of natural relaxation and provides a practical guide to techniques for enhancing mental and bodily self-awareness – the key to neuro-muscular relaxation and control.

The author presents two simple, daily programmes for reducing tension and coping calmly with the pressures of life. Separate chapters are devoted to rapid relaxation techniques, body posture and poise, promoting natural sleep and coping with emotional stress. Alternative techniques – including meditation, biofeedback, hypnosis and autogenic training – are also described. Throughout, the emphasis is on finding the techniques which work best for you in reducing anxiety and stress and promoting a healthier, more relaxed lifestyle.

Yoga

JAMES HEWITT

James Hewitt provides a clear and practical account of Hatha Yoga and Raja Yoga – the Yogas of bodily health and mental health respectively – whose regular practice produces greater energy, relaxation, poise and serenity.

The great value of this book is that the broader dimensions of Yoga are fully considered. A programme of Yoga postures and breathing exercises, and advice on relaxation and diet, are followed by a full consideration of Yoga meditation and its aims. Through regular Yoga practice and meditation you can attain greater vitality and suppleness, deep psycho-physical poise and relaxation, serenity and self-realisation.

'Most books on Yoga are either incoherent or incomprehensible or both, and there is an obvious need for something on the subject which is simple, clear, practical and short. This is such a book.'

The Times Educational Supplement